D0438917

The Fourth Medium

How to Use Promotional Literature to Increase Sales and Profits

The Fourth Medium

How to Use Promotional Literature to Increase Sales and Profits

Cameron S. Foote

DOW JONES-IRWIN
Homewood, Illinois   60430

This publication is designed to provide accurate and
authoritative information in regard to the subject matter
covered. It is sold with the understanding that the
publisher is not engaged in rendering legal, accounting, or
other professional service. If legal advice or other expert
assistance is required, the services of a competent
professional person should be sought.

*From a Declaration of Principles jointly adopted by a Committee
of the American Bar Association and a Committee of Publishers.*

ISBN 0-87094-913-6

Library of Congress Catalog Card No. 86–70966

Printed in the United States of America

1 2 3 4 5 6 7 8 9 0   MP   3 2 1 0 9 8 7 6

Promotional literature is simply
a printed way of differentiating
what you do, what you have, and how
you operate.

PREFACE

A few more years ago than I now care to remember, I was hired as an advertising assistant by one of the nation's largest corporations. The challenges and responsibilities of this entry-level position were to learn about the product line and its market through the preparation of promotional literature. It was a job for which only a general writing background had prepared me.

Specifically, my job was to write the brochures, booklets, and pamphlets that the company used to inform its representatives, dealers, and customers about its products.

The rationale was that by learning to sell the company's products through the use of the printed word, one became well grounded in the principles of marketing communications. And thus prepared, one could move on to the increasingly important tasks of managing sales promotion and advertising programs.

Certainly from a training standpoint the rationale was sound, for there was, indeed, no better way for myself and other newly hired advertising staff to be introduced and come to know intimately the company's products. And the feeling that only persons who knew and had written about the products could do a good job evaluating advertising copy and promotional programs in the future also had some merit.

However, from a marketing standpoint the program was seriously flawed. It put the primary responsibility for one of the most important and powerful components of the company's marketing communications effort into the hands of its least experienced personnel.

Within this company, as within many companies, the task of preparing promotional literature is done in-house, because it is felt that the detailed copy required of literature necessitates the type of in-depth product understanding only possible by an in-house staff. It is also felt to be less expensive to do it this way. And literature is not believed to need the creativity and impact of national ads and promotions anyway.

On the other hand, advertising and promotion programs are believed to need the type of specific expertise and professionalism which is difficult, if not impossible, to staff for internally. Thus, they can be handled more effectively by an outside agency.

The irony of this logic is that, while it is true that very specific advertising and promotional expertise is needed to create strong customer awareness, it is often literature that performs the next, and equally important marketing function—convincing the customer to purchase. This is especially true in business and industrial markets.

This means that literature needs every bit as much conceptual and executional professionalism as advertising copy. Literature which is not at least as effective in its role as the efforts which precede it are in theirs, can easily become the flawed link in an otherwise successful awareness-to-sales marketing cycle.

So, while it is true that literature created in-house usually costs less and is more precise in its details, it is also true that it often suffers from undisciplined thinking and uninspired creativity.

In short, it doesn't do the job very well.

This is not to argue that only an outside agency can produce good literature. Rather, it is to point out the obvious: Most companies and many agencies simply do not have the experience to do justice to literature—to give it the special budget and creative focus that it deserves.

If literature were an unimportant aspect of marketing with small budgets and not much riding on it wouldn't make much difference. But quite the opposite is actually true.

To illustrate, lets look at the company I once worked for— one of *Fortune* magazine's 25 largest industrial organizations and one regularly cited for its management's sophistication. Our product lines covered a variety of business and industrial markets. So each year we advertised in hundreds of trade magazines. Each year we also produced thousands of literature pieces of all types. And each year we spent almost one half of our communications budget on literature.

That's right, *nearly half of our multimillion dollar budget was spent on literature.* Yet, a casual observer would never know it, judging by the scant attention paid to literature preparation in memos and meetings. In fact, the two budget halves couldn't have been administered more differently. One—advertising—was subject to the most careful strategic planning and creative analysis. The other—literature—was subject only to strict purchasing control.

I've learned from two decades of subsequent experience that there is nothing unusual in this procedure. It is the norm, and it is only now beginning to change. Some agencies have set up groups with the express purpose of doing "collateral" materials, although one suspects this is often an attempt to justify the full-service agency concept. Some companies have become much more demanding and professional in what they expect their literature to accomplish.

Nonetheless, this remains virgin territory. No articles on the strategic importance of good literature appear in the *Harvard Business Review;* no articles on the creative approaches to good literature appear in *Advertising Age.* No creative seminars are given. This author is not aware of any other book on the subject.

So, the purpose of this book is twofold: 1) to provide the knowledge and understanding that managers need to assess the effectiveness of their organization's literature, and (2) to provide the guidelines that will help the creative staff—copywriters and designers—prepare the most effective literature for the communications task at hand. Put another way, the purpose of the book is to provide broad guidelines on what works, what doesn't work, and why.

The text is divided into the following sections. The Introduction tells why literature is a separate medium and should be treated as such. Part One gives the means for establishing a literature strategy. Part Two provides information on tactics for those producing literature, including specific creative tips for copywriters and designers. Part Three is a glossary that will be helpful not only to the novice, but also to the experienced individual as a reference guide. Part Four provides additional reference materials which will be particularly helpful for the less experienced, and for those wanting more specific information.

It is the assumption in this book that in most cases an organization's literature is used without other media support, a solitary effort devoted to explaining a position or product. When this is so, it provides the only information about a subject the reader will ever have.

In other cases, the literature may be part of a larger advertising campaign (collateral), it may be tied to a specific sales promotion, or it may be an element in a direct mail effort. When this is so, literature provides supplementary information, the amount determined by the primary medium.

In all cases, however, the literature's basic format and presentation, if not the content, are dictated by the needs and interests of the reader, and they don't change much. That's why it is possible to provide literature preparation and evaluation guidelines while recognizing that creativity is always hard to codify. And it's also why literature, while free to draw upon the elements which make good communication in the other three major promotional media—advertising, sales promotion and direct mail—is a medium unto itself.

The fourth medium.

Cameron S. Foote

ACKNOWLEDGMENTS

Writing a book to share knowledge gained over a professional lifetime is a wonderful undertaking. It is a catharsis, it makes you examine the most basic tenents of your profession, and it also forces you to learn many of the things you never had the time to learn before. Moreover, the demands and length of the process reawaken any humility that might have slipped into dormancy over the years.

To those readers who think they have a book in them, I highly recommend the experience. I especially recommend it if you have a patient editor to assure that your writing stay focused, and a smart agent like Dave Otte to guide you through the maze that is the publishing business. Their contributions to this manuscript are warmly appreciated and hereby publicly acknowledged.

I also want to publicly thank Robert Clark and Robert Rodin for their draft criticisms and suggestions, and the specific contributions of Robert McVoy and Marie McGinley.

Much more difficult to acknowledge are the hundreds of bosses, colleagues, and clients who have shared their wisdom with me over the years. Everything here first came from them. It is, of course, impossible to single them all out, but I would like to extend my thanks to two: John McAlister for giving me the break that everyone needs when starting out, and Adrian Van Dorpe for later providing the route to greater things.

CSF

INTRODUCTION

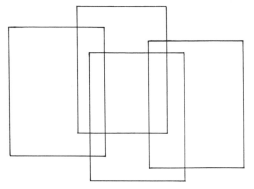

Promotional Literature: The Second Class Citizen of Mass Communication

Communication. What a positive word. And what portent. It conjures up images of exciting technologies and fast-growing, profitable industries.

But ask a politician what causes the world's problems and chances are he'll answer, "Failure to communicate." Likewise, ask a business executive about his or her concerns and chances are the answer will include compliance with government regulations, or personnel policies, or market research, or customer perceptions, or advertising, or salesmanship—all things affected by communication.

Communication remains a paradox: it is both the problem and the solution to much of what we like and dislike about our world. A major reason for this paradox is that every year we become more and more overcommunicated; we transmit more, we receive less.

The paradox really started with Gutenberg. Before he invented the means for mass communication, the problem was one with a few simple solutions: speak and write more clearly;

get the messenger a faster horse. Now, 500 years later, communications involves books, newspapers, magazines, mail, billboards, radio, TV, satellites, and computers, as well as the traditional human skills of speaking, listening, and writing. And for organizations large and small, commercial and noncommercial, communications also involves promotional literature—pamphlets, booklets, brochures, flyers, folders, stuffers, broadsides, and reports.

This book is about communicating with promotional literature. Specifically, it covers how to keep *your* promotional literature from adding to the communications glut by assuring that the messages conveyed are understood, believed, and remembered.

THE PROBLEMS OF ABUNDANCE

Certainly problems of abundance are psychologically easier to deal with than ones caused by scarcity. But that doesn't make them any easier to solve.

The extent to which the citizen of today is bombarded with communications messages would be mind-boggling to someone living even 100 years ago. Yet man has no more capacity to absorb and understand now than he had then. So he adapts by evolving the defense mechanism of ignoring all but the most informative, entertaining, or interesting.

The effect is that only a fraction of what we see and hear every day actually registers. And nearly all of what does register lacks credibility and is soon forgotten.

Because of this, new media and new techniques emerge every year. And the costs, particularly for the most dramatic and timely forms of communication, go up every year. Recently, TV commercials broke the $1 million-a-minute barrier for the first time. National magazine space can easily top $100,000 for a single insertion. Million dollar promotions and mailings are not uncommon.

With the stakes this high, the preparation of communications materials and the use of media have become a highly creative and professional business. It is a business that must blend art, craft, and commerce, and one that must constantly evolve and develop.

A hundred years ago posters and lithographs were the big medium. Then came the large, mass-circulation newspapers . . .

mass-circulation magazines . . . radio . . . TV . . . direct mail . . . cable. Each has been the hot medium for a time, but in the end each became just one more means of addressing our apparently insatiable need to communicate. Each new medium has created a potential for better communications while adding to the clutter.

Likewise, new techniques have come along, been popular and stylish, and have then receded to become just one more arrow in the communications quiver. Fine art . . . poetic words . . . salesmanship in print . . . market research . . . creative teaming . . . positioning . . . slice-of-life. Each is a technique; an effort to create attention, make a point, be memorable. In short, each is an effort to communicate better in an increasingly difficult environment.

Through all this, promotional literature, one of the oldest forms of mass communication, has also grown enormously in volume. The literature produced today is easily double the amount produced 10 years ago. Ask any printer. Ask any paper manufacturer. In fact, it sometimes seems, to paraphrase the British Field Marshall Montgomery, "The competitive wars won't end until the warring companies run out of paper."

Despite the growing importance and volume of promotional literature, there has been surprisingly little professional attention to either the strategies or the techniques employed. Today, in the mass communications priorities of most organizations, literature continues to place a distant fourth, being considered only after the advertising, sales promotion and direct mail strategies and budgets have been established. (The omission here of public relations is by design inasmuch as it is usually considered more of a craft or technique than a promotional medium.)

Promotional literature is the fourth, neglected medium. Given all the difficulty of communicating effectively in our overcommunicated society, that's unconscionable—unprofitable, too. Particularly since literature has some very strong communications advantages.

THE IMPORTANCE OF INDEPENDENCE

In a typical year, just the 1,500 companies listed on the New York Stock Exchange are said to introduce approximately 5,000 significant new products. In addition, tens of thousands of other companies introduce hundreds of thousands of new, improved, or modified products or services. To this is added countless organizations who disseminate information on countless subjects.

All these companies and organizations have the need to gain attention, to get through with a message. The result is an increasing problem in each of the three major media. It's called clutter. In advertising, viewers react to it by "zapping" commercials from what they watch and hear, and by skipping over the ads in what they read. In sales promotion, it shows in customer ennui which results in ignoring even the strongest offers. In direct mail, many mailings now go unopened because of the increasing perception that it's all just junk mail anyway.

Unfortunately, because each of these media utilize finite distribution channels, more activity just means more clutter and less impact. There are, after all, only so many publicly licensed frequencies and so many hours in the day. There are only so many newsstands available for distribution, just so many counters for promotions, and a limited number of mailboxes. It's a catch 22: The more we say, the more difficult it is to get an ear. Yet we know that in communications more always results in less.

What to do about clutter? In every market the answer is to select media with the narrowest audience segmentation possible and combine it with the most attention-getting creativity—a *rifle shot* approach with strong memorability. The rationale is this: If your message is addressed to the specialized interests of a small, carefully defined audience, chances are enough of them will note it to make it productive. If your message is also combined with strong creativity—the type that makes an audience notice, remember, and desire—the results can be dynamite.

Literature is the ultimate segmentable medium. That's because its distribution is uncontrolled and can be unlimited. One or millions of copies can be produced. They can be distributed individually or in bulk, over the counter or by mail. One or hundreds of pages can be used. There are no editorial constraints or environments to consider, no deadlines not self-imposed. A piece can stand by itself, or supplement another communications effort as collateral. And because it is independent of the timetables set by others, it can also be available at the precise time when it will have the most impact.

Alone among the media, literature can be anything the originator wants. It can be as pointed and direct, as broad and indirect, as fancy or plain, or as timely as necessary to get the job done.

THE ADVANTAGES OF BUDGET FLEXIBILITY

Because of all of the above, literature can also be as expensive or as inexpensive as the job requires, or as the budget allows. There is no minimum expenditure necessary to insure effectiveness. Nor are there minimum creative standards or production values necessary to assure impact.

This flexibility makes literature the only mass communications medium that can be utilized by organizations of all sizes. Local charities and mom-and-pop stores, international corporations and nonprofit organizations—all can use it. It is the most democratic of the media.

It is also the only form of mass communication that can work equally well for all. As previously stated, it does not require sufficient expenditure to overcome some threshold of awareness. There is also no need for the repetition which benefits those who advertise more frequently; every literature piece more or less stands on its own merits.

A small company with a limited budget to communicate the benefits of a new product may elect only to produce a single data sheet. Whereas in a large organization a similar data sheet may be the smallest part of an extensive communications campaign which includes broadcast commercials, print ads, direct mailings, in-store promotions, and billboards. Nonetheless, whether as a solo effort or part of a campaign, both data sheets will be equally as effective.

THE BENEFITS OF BEING DESIRED

The other mass communications media have a disadvantage which they must constantly overcome: they are intrusive and disruptive. Mr. Average American watching TV at night looks upon commercials as an annoyance; the reader of the morning paper grumbles about the quantity of ads; the weekly shopper complains about in-store promotions getting in the way; a mailbox filled each day with mailers is almost as great a disappointment as one filled with bills.

In most cases the individual acknowledges and accepts the intrusion as the price paid in our society for free entertainment, relatively unbiased news, and a plethora of choices. Yet it is an acceptance that is always made grudgingly.

Because of this, organizations must constantly strive to make their media efforts entertaining, or newsworthy, or otherwise stylistically fitting with the medium they are using. In doing so, of course, some portion of the time or space is always spent in the noncommunication function of winning over or placating the viewer. This is especially noticeable in TV, where up to half a commercial's time can be used to set the stage for the real message. Nonetheless, it is necessary because it is the only way to overcome the built-in disadvantage of the medium.

None of the above is necessarily true with literature. It is seldom disruptive or intrusive; mostly it is picked up and read voluntarily because the reader *wants* the information it contains. It has, in short, a unique characteristic among the media—desirability.

THE OPPORTUNITIES FOR THE FUTURE

No other medium can offer the communicator the preceding three advantages: independence, budget flexibility, and desirability.

Of course, it would be ludicrous to suggest that nothing else is needed, that literature could ever be a replacement for a well-conceived and -executed advertising campaign, sales promotion program, or direct mailing. Even under the most ideal circumstances, literature can never achieve the transmittal speed, the distribution reach and frequency, or the tremendous impact of the three other media. Yet not to consider literature as a vital, coordinated part of the marketing mix is to seriously reduce both communications effectiveness and efficiency. It is a big mistake made much too often, especially in light of what we can project about the future.

Economic Trends

Today, our society is being propelled by what has been described as the most revolutionary economic change in a century: the emergence of a new economy in which services and high technology play dominant roles. Some call it the equivalent of a new industrial revolution.

In this new economic order, communications programs must change if they are to continue to be effective. Services, which by their very nature are much less precise and harder to define than products, require media exposure that goes beyond merely calling attention to a few benefits; detailed explanation is also necessary. Moreover, this is as true for consumer services as it is for business and industrial services. For example, take the selling of lawn care, one of the fastest-growing of today's consumer services. It relies on all traditional media to get leads, but on literature to explain exactly what will be done and when.

Likewise, in the future it will become more and more necessary for organizations and individuals to understand all the ramifications of any technology being acquired, as opposed to merely understanding its less important features and immediate benefits. Many technologies require a commitment to a system which can have profound implications on future operations and purchases. This is very evident in computer hardware with proprietary operating systems, and in the fundamental differences between computer software packages performing the same basic functions.

In addition, many technological products also do so much, in so many different ways, that understanding their potential is necessary in order to make an informed purchasing decision. Again, while the implications of this are much greater to business and industry, it is also of concern to the consumer marketer. Whereas it was once easy for a consumer to pick out a product such as a radio, based on nothing more than a brand name, now the selection of stereo components involves a complex set of motivations, most of which necessitate detailed information in some form. Consider videocassette recorders (VCRs), for example.

In these new environments, the three traditional media will continue to be of dominant importance. But literature will become of increasing importance overall, and will dominate certain market segments. It is ironic that an information age ushered in by technology will find one of the oldest forms of providing information—printed promotional literature—so increasingly necessary.

Social Trends

Economic and social trends go hand-in-hand, of course. The advances of technology, the availability of information, and the ease of communication have wrought profound change. They have made our world smaller, more open and less structured, although not necessarily more just. Combined with a number of other complex forces, they have also helped provide more economic opportunity to more people.

For the foreseeable future, this much is irreversible: Each year there will be more people making more informed decisions, and fewer people relying upon intuition and tradition. Individuals will live longer, become ever better educated, and move about more often. In addition, each year more women and minorities will move to positions of responsibility.

These changes are worldwide in scope if not equal everywhere in intensity. They come about largely as a result of the explosion of information that marks our age. There is no turning back, for information is a self-intensifying spiral: The more one wants to know, the more there is to know. And the more needs are identified, and the narrower the interests, the more promotional literature becomes an appropriate and economical means to address them.

To this long-term and irreversible trend has recently been added something more contemporaneous, but also very powerful. It is the strong resurgence throughout much of the world, but particularly in the United States, of the basic values of capitalism. This means not only increased emphasis on a free market economy, but also the necessity, indeed the obligation, for an individual to make economic choices and be responsible for them. Only history will tell whether this is a temporary aberration, or a long-term reversal of the trend towards governmental policies that control and reduce economic choices.

Whatever the case, it is inescapable that today we live in

a society where capitalist values have the strongest influence of any time since the 1920s. The evidence is everywhere. Our cultural heroes are increasingly drawn from the ranks of young, aggressive entrepreneurs. Conspicuous consumption is accepted. Acquiring and owning is more often done for its own sake, not always to serve some utilitarian function. Moreover, all this appears to be true in relatively bad times, as well as good.

To relate this trend to our subject matter, today the fastest-growing, most contested markets are for considered purchases of premium goods and services. And this is precisely the area in which promotional literature has the strongest impact and is most cost-efficient.

Communications Trends

At a time when the marketplace is more service- and technology-oriented, and when consumption is more valued, there are also more people every year who want to use the available promotional media.

Today, the value of persuasive communications is never seriously questioned, as it was as little as a generation ago. Now, the only debates arise over effective use. Nearly every organization, large and small, uses some sort of promotional media to tell its story.

Even the last holdouts, the professions, are no longer immune. Because there are more physicians relative to the size of the population than ever before, they face an increasing need to differentiate themselves from their colleagues. Moreover, individual physicians, for whom most traditional promotional techniques are either legally or ethically proscribed, face tremendous competitive pressure from health maintenance organizations (HMOs) and neighborhood clinics. Both advertise and promote extensively.

Likewise, the lawyer population is more than twice as large as it was just 15 years ago. At the same time, many restrictions on promotion have been lifted by state bar associations. Any new lawyer seeking to establish a viable practice today knows that he or she must consider using some means of persuasive mass communication.

For both these professions, as well as for dentists, engineers, educators, psychologists, chiropractors, and consultants, literature is usually the most attractive medium, and sometimes the only appropriate medium. It can provide a scholarly yet persuasive means to set a single professional apart from his/her colleagues. It does not have the overt promotional flavor of the other media. It is usually less expensive. And it is far more flexible and long lasting.

In addition, continuing pressure on communications media comes from government deregulation of some of America's larger industries; telecommunications and transportation are two prime examples. Each time controls are lifted from an industry, hundreds of millions of dollars are immediately pumped into the promotional media in a quick attempt to establish or protect a market position. Although initially advertising intensive, in many cases the stories which must be ultimately told—especially to larger customers and the financial community—can only be handled by literature.

All of this points not only to a continued growth of all communications media, but to a disproportionately high growth rate for promotional literature.

THE BOTTOM LINE

The number of organizations which use literature will continue to grow. The amount they spend each year on literature will continue to grow. And the relative importance of literature as a communications medium will continue to grow. Yet, most of the literature produced today is not subject to management scrutiny. It fulfills no defined need, is not creatively sound, looks amateurish; and is far too expensive; or all of the above. For some reason, literature has thus far managed to elude the professionalism that has made the other three promotional media— advertising, sales promotion and direct mail—so highly effective. It is discriminated against because of its lack of professionalism, and it lacks professionalism because it is discriminated against.

Now, that must change. Given the money involved and the potential that's at stake, second class citizenship for promotional literature is a condition that an organization can no longer afford to tolerate.

It's time that the potential of the medium was understood, benchmarks established for determining need, standards adopted for judging performance, and guidelines established for helping to prepare what works best.

It's time the second class citizen of mass communication also came of age.

CONTENTS

Part Two—Tactics for Producing Good Literature

Part Four—Appendixes

Part One

Establishing a Literature Strategy

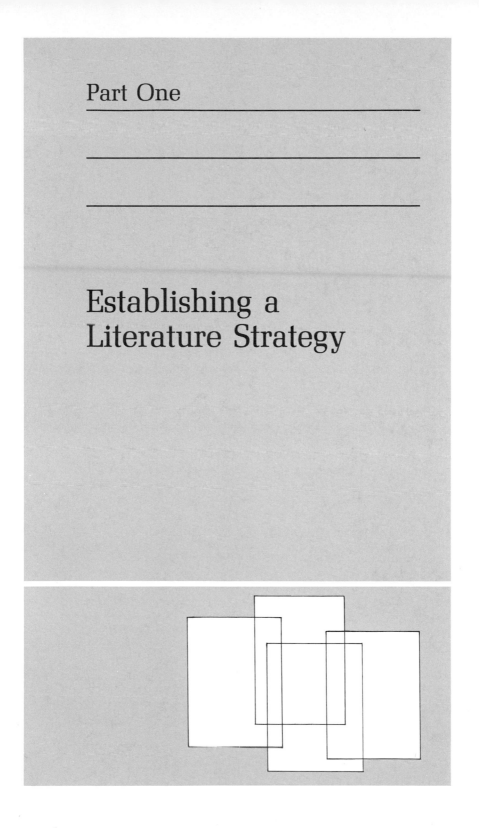

CHAPTER 1

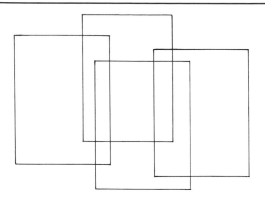

Defining the Medium

As technology has provided ever more economical means of mass communications, the disciplines surrounding each of the media used have become increasingly well defined and understood. Most readers of this book will have a good understanding of what "advertising," "sales promotion" and "direct mail" are and how they are used. If not, short definitions can be found in the Glossary, and each is the subject of numerous texts.

Unfortunately, an understanding of promotional literature is not as universal, so we must start with a definition. As the term will be used here, it means all stand-alone and self-contained printed materials that one party or group uses to communicate with another.

Obviously, that definition covers a lot of diverse material. And there is also considerable overlap with the other media. For example, is a booklet bound into a magazine considered literature, or is it an ad? Is a flyer contained in a point-of-purchase display actually sales promotion? Is an envelope-sized stuffer actually direct mail? Does it matter?

Probably not. The problem with definitions in the communications business is that they are antithetical to the whole creative process upon which the business is founded. Moreover, too often they are taken literally and not used as they should be: as a starting point for doing better, more effective work. So, let's also make it plain that the above definition is provided here only as a reference, a way of identifying those materials that have similar communications potential and that respond to similar creative methods. It is not intended to exclude anything.

Having such a definition does, however, allow us to organize printed materials into two groups: one which contains items which are conceived, written and designed to exist on their own, independent of any other medium; and another which contains items primarily designed as part of another medium. Because the latter is covered adequately in books on the other media, what follows concentrates primarily on the former.

With the definition out of the way, then, we can now turn to those things that make promotional literature a separate and distinct medium.

THE THREE THINGS THAT MAKE LITERATURE DIFFERENT

As discussed in the introduction, literature is usually the fourth (last) medium in many organizations' communications priorities. It is never that low in terms of its ability to actually impact decision making, but it is nonetheless true that it is nearly always secondary or tertiary to other efforts. In most cases literature functions in an environment of perceptions already created by an individual, by an ad, or by a variety of sources and media over the years.

1. *That something or someone has nearly always preceded literature to create a perception or an awareness is the most important difference between this medium and the others.* More than any other thing, the fact that the reader already has an impression or an idea, however slight, affects in every aspect the strategy and the creativity with which a literature project should be approached. For example, in other media there is an ongoing need to create awareness for new messages, so new ways must be constantly found to attract attention and to create memorability. This, in turn, puts a heavy premium on those skills which evoke emotion and provide entertainment and which associate a particular message with a particular mood, event, or person. Seldom is this the case with literature.

2. *Providing detail is the second major difference between literature and other media.* Because literature functions to either reinforce or attempt to change already established perceptions and ideas, its purpose, first and foremost, is to provide convincing detail. It is not enough for literature to simply create a good impression or plant an idea. It must always go the next step and provide credible proof.

None of the other media provide an affordable, open-ended way to organize and present the myriad of facts and arguments that are often necessary to motivate someone to action. While it is possible in many cases to motivate an individual to action without detail (e.g., purchasers of low-price commodity items), it is also true that most important decisions require reflection and consideration. Only literature provides the means to marshal the facts and present a convincing, permanent argument.

3. *More than any other form of communication, literature reflects an organization.* It is seldom affected by third-party-imposed formats, deadlines, and deliveries. There are few if any physical constraints, no editorial or other environments to consider, no restrictions on timing. Because of all of these things, literature can have a very long life.

This means that literature, unlike other media, can be anything an organization desires. It also means, in turn, that it always reflects the organization's style and thinking. Other media, ads and mailers for example, do create impressions of an organization, but in most cases what's created is affected by the media used, is task oriented, and is ephemeral. Only literature assumes the continuous role of a silent employee: a surrogate representative working independently, around the clock, delivering an organization's message where it is impossible or impractical for humans. If it's done well it reflects positively on the organization, much like a good sales force. If not, it reflects negatively, like a bad sales force.

CONDUCTING THE GENERAL ANALYSIS

All organizational activity benefits from an objective analysis of the specific job to be done and the resources that can be applied to accomplish it. However, there should also be a step before this. Relying on an analysis of specific needs or resources only to determine literature requirements has the potential to do far more harm than good. Also needed is a more general analysis. It must take into account the position of the organization or product in the marketplace, as well as the present and future activity of the other communications media.

While literature takes the tangible form of individual pieces of printed material, actually it is a process that also heavily affects, and is affected by, the other media and the environment (market) in which it will be used. Thus, the real value of literature can only be determined when it is analyzed as part of a larger communications plan.

Putting together such a plan should start with the compilation of information on market needs. Then a set of objectives for meeting these needs should be defined. Finally, the communications resources which will make meeting the needs possible should be determined. If all this is done well (exactly how is a process adequately detailed in countless other books) the result will be a communications plan that is both objective and effective.

The validity of the communications plan that emerges from this process can be tested in three ways. It should be: (1) reasonable—worthwhile in terms of needs and costs; (2) attainable—capable of being accomplished; and (3) measurable—trackable in terms of progress. When the plan meets these requirements, the role of literature in it can be much more objectively determined.

The perceived need for literature in the communications plan should now be evaluated in light of one or more of three criteria. These criteria are an extension of the three things that make literature different from other media, as covered above.

The first of these differences, and the first one that should be considered in a general analysis, is that literature nearly always operates in an environment where the reader is already familiar with the product or service. Thus: *The first criterion for determining the need for literature is whether any additional information is necessary to produce, or hasten, a decision or action by the reader.*

If so, how much and with what broadness of distribution? For example, does a potential customer already know enough to make an immediate purchasing decision? Has all the convincing necessary for a decision already been done? Is the customer's mind made up? In all these cases, literature will be a waste of money.

On the other hand, how many more products would be sold if literature were available? Could the consideration time be reduced? Might literature now affect a decision later? Could other media costs be reduced? Would fewer salespersons be necessary? And to what extent?

The second difference between literature and the other media is its ability to provide convincing detail. Thus: *The second criterion for determining the need for literature is whether more detail than can be delivered by salespeople or other media is necessary for a decision or action by the reader.*

Is there any real need for lengthy descriptions, persuasive arguments, specifications, or illustrations? Just as important, is there need for consideration over time, or in places where salespeople or other media are not present? Do other people in the organization, who cannot be reached by salespeople or other media, need detail to make informed decisions?

The third difference between literature and the other media is the unique way in which it reflects an organization. Thus: *The third criterion for determining the need for literature is whether insight into the organization's personality and style are necessary for a decision or action by the reader.*

Or does the reader simply make a decision based on the way a few facts or features meet the perceived requirements?

This consideration is not to be confused with the sophistication with which the literature is ultimately prepared. That subject will come up later. Rather, here the point to consider is whether there is a need to go beyond detail and information to give a feeling for those intangible elements that are best described collectively as style. In other words, is it necessary for the medium to become part of the message?

Because so much literature is produced automatically, without thought, it can't be stressed strongly enough here that *only when one or more of these three criteria have been met should the production of any literature be considered—for any purpose.* In other words, that the requirements of step one should always be met before going on to step two.

Only after being satisfied through this process that there is a need for literature of some type, is it important to consider step two—what that type should be. This is done by matching the specific need to the literature type which best addresses it.

CONSIDERING THE JOB TO BE DONE

It is important now to do an objective analysis of the specific need to be addressed. In doing this, remember that literature use is just one step in a much larger process called communication. This communication process has four distinct phases whenever it is used commercially to inform or persuade. These four phases, outlined below, not only determine whether a product or idea is bought or accepted, but often determine as well the chances for repeated success.

Awareness is the first phase, during which the individual becomes cognizant of the communications message, but doesn't make a decision as to whether it is interesting enough for further consideration.

Questioning, the second phase, follows either literally or figuratively for the individual who has expressed interest. It is the time when concerns are brought to the surface, when facts are evaluated. Information received during this phase often determines what decision is made.

Deciding is the third decision-making phase. From a combination of facts, interests, prejudices, and influences a course of action will be chosen. The proposition will be accepted, the product bought. Or it will be rejected.

Contentment/unhappiness, the fourth phase, happens after the fact. Was the decision made the right one? Or, based on what has become known, was it a mistake? If I had it to do over again, would I?

Every individual who is the recipient of a message designed to persuade him/her to buy or take action should be led through these four distinct phases, step by step. To the extent that this does not happen, the communications process has broken down, probably due to the communicator's ineffectual strategy, creativity, or materials.

It is also important to consider that the four phases are usually separate and distinct from one another, and, most important for our purposes, that they are usually best addressed by a different combination of media. Literature can play a strong role in three of the four.

The Role of Literature in Creating Awareness. Certainly the most difficult of the four phases of communications is gaining and sustaining awareness. It is also the most important, for without it, nothing happens. This is the reason why billions of dollars are spent each year on all forms of advertising—broadcast, space, outdoor, reminder, etc.

Although it is possible for literature to create awareness, it is usually far too expensive on a cost-per-contact basis to be cost effective. The reason for this is twofold: First is the tremendous efficiency with which emotion and entertainment can create and sustain awareness. The mass media (particularly TV) provide the best, most efficient environment to do this. Second, when printed materials are used to build awareness, as in direct mail, they must be carefully structured to attract interest quickly and tell a story simply. This structure is poles opposite from that of good literature, which must present detail, and/or provide the reasoned, persuasive argument that is necessary for most considered purchases.

In short, literature, again as defined by its difference from other printed materials, is seldom very effective in this first phase of the communication process. Rather, it is better used, indeed can play a central role, in the three additional steps which are usually necessary to make a sale, change a mind, and assure repeat business.

The Role of Literature in Answering Questions. Literature is used more in this capacity than in any other. It is the ideal follow-up medium to take the awareness created by advertising, word of mouth, or past reputation, and move it along to the decision-making phase. It does this by providing specific answers to questions, by overcoming conscious and subconscious objections, and by providing needed specifications and detail.

All types of literature can be used for this purpose, although some are better suited than others. Instruction books, for example, although occasionally used before a sale to provide detailed facts and specifications, would probably be very expensive and not very effective in general use. At the other end of the scale, bill stuffers would be ideal for recalling features mentioned in an ad, but would probably be ineffective when information must be provided before a customer makes a considered purchase.

Which type of literature is best for a specific use depends upon several factors, the most important being the amount of information needed by the reader to come to a decision, the efficiency of the awareness medium in pre-disposing a reader toward action, and the receptivity of the reader.

Whichever type is selected, however, it is critically important to remember that the role of literature here is to provide whatever additional information and assurance is necessary for the reader to get from the awareness to the decision-making phase as expeditiously as possible. In short, to provide a strong bridge from one activity to the other.

Instead, too often, literature is hastily produced without proper consideration of this important role. This is most often seen, although by no means exclusively, in the tendency to treat much product literature as "collateral"—that is, a mere extension of an advertising message.

The Role of Literature in Decision Making.   There is considerable overlap between literature used to provide answers to reader questions, and that used to help readers reach a decision. In many cases, they are one and the same. In fact, literature designed specifically for this latter purpose is usually only appropriate in those cases where there is personal salesmanship, or where there is a very specific opportunity to affect a decision at point of sale.

In both these cases, decision-making literature can provide a strong, additional stimulus that can make the difference between closing a sale and losing it. Thus, it probably should be part of an organization's literature mix whenever appropriate.

Presentation materials, for example, are often very valuable in providing a summary of benefits which will help a salesperson get a commitment on the spot. Counter literature can substantially increase impulse purchases. And product stickers and tags can tip the sales balance between two similar products.

This is what can happen. Whether it will or not depends upon many factors, not the least of which is the skill of presentation, as discussed in Chapter 4. However, for the purpose of analyzing whether such literature will be effective for a specific product, consider that it is one of the few types of promotion whose effectiveness can be easily tested. If you have the opportunities mentioned above, try literature for six months. If sales go up by a substantial factor, continue; if not, stop.

The Role of Literature in Assuring Contentment, Defusing Unhappiness.   Every organization wants the various publics with which it deals to be contented after the sale. Although this is partly out of pride and chauvinism, usually the reason is also very pragmatic: a happy customer comes back for more, and helps to build the reputation that can become an organization's single most valuable asset.

There is, of course, no question that personal contact is the most effective way of making this happen. But there is also no question that personal contact, whether through a service representative or toll-free telephone number, can be expensive. It should be used no more than necessary and may not be warranted for many less expensive products and services. Even at best, personal service doesn't have the immediacy that is sometimes important.

What's needed is an always-available, straightforward, detailed source of information and assistance that can be used on a daily basis or in case anything goes wrong.

Literature can do this very effectively. At the same time it can also express thanks to the customer for selecting the product or service. It can be the cheapest possible way to affect customer satisfaction after the sale.

At its simplest, this literature can take the form of a thank you or warranty card with information on how to obtain service;

at its most complex it can be a detailed instruction manual. Usually something in between, related to the complexity of the product or service, is appropriate. However, regardless of form, some type of help literature should be included in every packaged product and made available as part of most service offerings.

CHAPTER 2

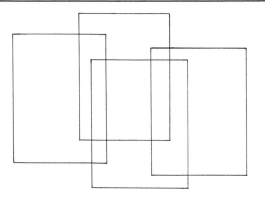

Determining Needs and Setting a Budget

          A dilemma in any communications planning process is whether to start with a budget and attempt to tailor a plan to match it, or start by compiling a list of needs and use it as the basis for determining a budget. Generally, the former approach works best for highly structured, regular activities with past management or industry practices to draw upon; the latter for less-structured activities with a shorter history of management attention. In nearly all cases, promotional literature falls into this latter category.

    Although planning and budgeting through first compiling a list of needs involves examining more options and is more work, it presents many more opportunities.

    In the first section of this chapter, we'll take up the subject of determining literature needs. The second section will then deal with budgeting and literature cost effectiveness.

DETERMINING NEEDS

The First, and Usually Most Important, Consideration in Determining Literature Needs Is Distribution.   How much circulation is necessary? Will the literature be provided to everyone in a certain group, be made widely available through a large dealer network, or controlled through a small sales force? And what is a reasonable expectation of its impact? Will it take an average of one piece to produce two orders, or one piece for 200 orders? Or perhaps there is no immediate sales function, just long-term information.

The best source for these and other answers is to look at the organization's past experience. Then, to the extent that it can be determined, to look at what other, similar organizations do, especially competitors. In both cases, however, keep in mind that what has been done in the past may not necessarily have been the right thing to do. Literature distribution is not a subject with much objective decision making, so it is always wise to temper past experience with present common sense.

The other major source of distribution input is the perceived needs of the actual users. If distribution is through a sales force or dealer network, their stated requirements must be factored in. Here again, however, this input should be tempered by the fact that there is a vested interest, especially if the literature is free, to inflate the types and quantities needed. Even so, it should never appear to those working in the field that their input is disregarded, even if the needs seem unreasonable. Always remember that one of the functions literature performs is a visible show of sales support. The value of literature as a merchandising tool as well as a sales tool should never be underestimated.

This evaluation of distribution requests and history should provide the first indication of literature needs. It should then be refined by the three other considerations that follow.

The Second Consideration Is Where in the Communications Cycle the Literature Will Be Used.   Will the literature be used before, at the time of, or following a sale or decision? For example, literature designed to create awareness will have to be produced in very large quantities to have any chance at effectiveness. At the other end of the scale, literature produced to assure contentment, such as instruction books, can be very effective when produced in quantities only slightly greater than that of the product.

The effective quantities of decision-making literature are always tied to the number of personal contacts or purchasing outlets. And the quantities of literature designed to answer questions should be inversely proportional to the degree to which the product features and benefits are already known.

New products and ideas also need much more literature support than mature ones. First of all, there is a literature distribution pipeline to fill. Chances are there will be initial sales or other pressure that will call for the use of large amounts of literature. Most important, the very fact of newness usually defines a product or idea as an unknown. The purpose of all communication, including literature, is to make the unknown, known.

Once distribution requirements are determined they should be reviewed in light of exactly where in the communications process the literature fits. In addition, there should be a plan formulated to reduce the future needs for the literature as the product or idea moves inevitably from being new through to maturity.

The Third Consideration Is How Long the Literature Can Remain Current. For literature to be effective, the reader must always believe it is up to date. This is no problem for literature designed for one-time use. But for literature carried in inventory, major consideration should be given to maintaining its currency.

For mature products or ideas, currency will probably be more a function of style and appearance than of content. For evolving products or ideas, however, it will probably be directly related to accuracy—correct strategy, proper descriptions, and the latest specifications.

Obviously, the newer a product or idea is, the more often changes will be necessary in the literature to keep it effective. Conversely, the older and more stable it is, the less often literature changes will be necessary.

As a general rule of thumb, between six months and two years of supply should be printed. At least six months worth is needed to support introductory products and new ideas, and up to two years worth to support stable, mature products and ideas. Most needs fall somewhere in between.

A six-month supply is needed because of the time required to fill the inventory pipeline, and the wisdom of avoiding any of the confusion that can result from information that is changed too often. At the other end of the scale, it is seldom wise to exceed a two-year supply because the risk of obsolescence is too great, and the cost of carrying inventory without periodic review is too expensive.

The Fourth Consideration Is Everything Else.   From careful consideration of distribution requirements, past experience, the communications cycle, and the need for periodic change, a first cut can be made at determining what literature is needed, and in what quantities. At this time, however, there are several other factors which should also be considered.

One is a printing trade custom, thankfully not as much of a problem now as in the past, which permits delivery and billing of a quantity 10 percent over or under that which is ordered. This is to accommodate the variability of spoilage which can be encountered in the multioperation printing production process. Because of it, the only way to assure a specific quantity is to order 10 percent more than needed, in case the press run comes up 10 percent short. Normally, the result, of course, is to receive 20 percent more than needed. (Their 10 percent overage, plus your 10 percent insurance quantity.) Printing trade customs are detailed in Appendix Two.

Also, any accumulated back orders must be considered for literature that is being updated, or has been preannounced.

The popularity factor for new literature must be taken into account, too. As in any creative endeavor, some things are more popular and, thus, in higher demand than others. Newness helps. For example, a new, particularly well-done corporate capability brochure may find uses far beyond the initial requirement for sales support. While it is very difficult to predict such things in advance, they should be considered.

In addition, since no individual literature piece operates in a vacuum, the effects of any one on all others must be considered. Indeed, unless the organization is growing in both size and financial strength, the goal of a well-run literature program should be that every new literature piece replaces an existing one. In short, nothing new is added without something old being deleted.

Finally, the determination of literature needs should be done by a very few individuals, ideally one person. While many sources should be solicited and many ideas considered, there should be only one source for decisions. That source should be the individual(s) with budget responsibility who will make the final determination of literature needs based on cost-effectiveness criteria such as those following.

SETTING A BUDGET

Unlike such other media as advertising, there is no data or norm on what level of expenditure is appropriate for literature in a given type of industry or organization.

As a general guideline, industrial organizations, which sell proportionally more high-ticket, considered-purchase items, have the highest literature budgets. They often match, and sometimes exceed, advertising budgets. Consumer-oriented industries have the lowest relative literature budgets, a fraction of advertising expenditures. Service organizations fall anywhere in between.

On a cost-per-contact basis, literature also has the widest range of any medium. It can be mere pennies for a bill stuffer that reaches hundreds of thousands of potential customers over retail counters, or hundreds of dollars for a presentation book used only a few times to help explain a complicated program to key decision makers. And because there are no external constraints placed on literature as there are in other media (such as the space and time units of advertising), there are no industry benchmarks for size or style to rely upon.

In addition, there are also no cost-per-thousand (CPM) figures, readership reports, or audience share data to refer to in determining the most effective placement of literature.

Despite the lack of these financial management tools, there are, nonetheless, strong guidelines for establishing a literature budget. These same guidelines can also help establish whether an existing literature program is operating in the most cost-effective and beneficial way for an organization.

What Best Matches the Need? This may sound more elementary than it really is. Too often literature preparation is simply an automatic response: a selling brochure is seen as necessary for every new product; a newsletter is required to match a competitor's; a new capability brochure must be redone to show organizational changes. Because of this type of automatic response, up to half of all literature produced is probably inappropriate and wasteful for the job it should be doing. Perhaps some other type of literature can do the job just as well.

As in any creative endeavor, it is better to have done a few things really well, that deliver strong impact, than to do many things that have minimal impact and effectiveness. This does not necessarily mean doing things in the most expensive way. It would, for example, probably be a mistake to print expensive multipage selling brochures for primary use in discount outlets. Small stuffers would fit the environment better and tell the story faster. Conversely, the cheapest way is not always appropriate either. The use of poorly prepared stuffers to describe expensive products sold through specialty shops is equally inappropriate.

The most efficient literature is always that which is written, designed, illustrated, and printed in the way that best matches the product, its market and the other media being used.

Where Is the Product in Its Life Cycle?   Like people, all products (and services and ideas) go through a life cycle from young, to mature, to aging, to dying. Although with products it is possible to prolong this cycle (sometimes extensively) through various marketing and communications skills, in the end, everything ends.

Generally, the newer the product is, the bigger the literature budget needed; the older it is, the smaller the literature budget. Therefore, in determining how much money is appropriate to spend on literature for a particular product, it is necessary to consider where it is in its life cycle.

For example, for the introduction of a significant product many types of literature may be initially appropriate in order to assure market interest. Then, as the product matures, the literature list can perhaps be pared to include only a few items to sustain that interest, such as a selling brochure, stuffer, and catalog listing. Later, as the product ages, perhaps only a couple of items to answer inquiries, such as a stuffer and catalog listing, will be appropriate. Finally, as the product nears the end of its life, perhaps all that will be necessary is a catalog listing for ordering.

Likewise, the elaborateness of each of the literature pieces used, and the amount of detail they include, can probably be reduced as they are reprinted over the life cycle of the product

In determining a total literature budget that covers many products, the net effect of the constantly changing ages of the products in the line must also be considered. In a year with proportionately more new products, the yearly budget would usually be higher; it would usually be lower if the proportion of older products increased. And, unless the profit margin is rising, the overall literature budget should not normally increase if the proportion of older products to newer products remains about the same.

What Is Reasonable?   It would be helpful if there were spending norms to refer to (for example, expenditure as a percent of sales) but they don't exist for literature. The only guidelines are those you'll establish, and perhaps the best is expenditure against return (margin) for each individual product or idea.

In this approach, every literature need is considered independently, and adding all needs together results in the overall literature budget.

The reason this approach works so well for literature is that, unlike other media where certain expenditures are justified in order to sustain a general awareness, literature always has a very specific task related to an individual product or idea. This means that the expenditure on each literature piece has to be totally justified in its contribution to either the profitability or acceptance of its subject.

To help determine how much expenditure is reasonable, consider three factors: image, competition, and cost.

What is the image presented by the other promotional media? Whatever it is, chances are the literature should be complementary in its quality (cost). An expensive advertising campaign supported by cheap sales brochures produced after the promotional budget has been depleted is obviously self-defeating. Equally self-defeating is elaborately prepared instructional material in cheap product packaging. The more all inclusive and coordinated a marketing or communications plan is, the easier it will be to determine how much money is too little, and how much is too much.

What is the competition doing? Literature never operates in a competitive vacuum. Your literature should be better, although not necessarily more expensive, than that provided for competitive products. When used in conjunction with better advertising and better packaging, better literature helps create the superior market position that can lower the cost of sales, and allow higher prices and better margins. It is difficult, if not impossible, to ascertain a reasonable literature expenditure without knowing what the competition is up to.

Is it affordable? For products, start by looking at the gross margin projected without any literature support. Then, consider how many more sales will be generated when supported by the literature planned. Will the cost of the literature be more than 60 percent of the incremental revenue? If so, take a hard look at its need. When looking at anything nonquantifiable, like ideas, consider how much the literature will cost and divide that by the people it will reach. Is getting the idea across really that important? In every case, temper your analysis with a dash of common sense, too. Will, for example, scrimping on literature increase servicing expenses, or alienate critical dealers?

In short, a reasonable literature expenditure is simply the lowest amount that does the job required.

Can Costs Be Better Managed?   Continuity, quality, professionalism, and economies of scale all argue for as few sources of literature creativity and budgeting as possible within an organization. At the same time, however, it is wise to have a system that allocates at least part of the costs of literature to those who directly benefit from its use.

The management advantages of centralized control should be self-evident. Not so immediately apparent, or as widely practiced, is the advantage of decentralizing the accounting. Combining both is a way of increasing cost-effectiveness which has unfortunately eluded many organizations.

Allocating costs can ease the pressure on sensitive budgets. It can also help assure a more accurate tally of the actual costs associated with a product or idea. And it can act as a very effective test of real need.

Allocation can be by product, profit center, or distribution channel. For example, departments can be charged for all literature produced for them, or field representatives can be charged a unit cost for literature ordered. It has been said that since such cross-charges are only "internal money," they result only in higher administrative costs without a corresponding increase in income. However, experience shows that they also invariably result in a significant reduction of costly waste.

The same effect holds true externally. Although it can be expensive to set up a system to charge dealers and agents for literature, it can also pay off in the long run. The key to success is establishment of minimal, "share-cost" prices which are high enough to discourage waste, but low enough not to alienate dealers or discourage legitimate literature use. No effort should be made to turn literature into a profit center. Indeed, an organization should count itself fortunate if the money collected from the charges will cover administrative costs. The real effect on the bottom line will come from lower costs over the long run.

What Happens If You Cut Back?   Maybe nothing. So perhaps it is worth a try. There is a general rule in sailing that holds that a boat should keep trying to sail closer to the wind until its sails just start to flap, then to back off just enough to keep its sails full. So it is with literature. The right literature budget is probably an amount just above the point of declining effect. This won't necessarily be easy to determine, but, chances are, little harm will be done in trying if cutbacks are gradual and the results are well monitored.

Unlike most other media in which each new effort builds upon what went before to create long-term effects, most literature affects only the immediate acceptance of a single product or idea. Therefore, it is easy to experiment without potentially disastrous results.

One way to start is to set a limit on the amount of new literature that will be supplied to representatives and dealers. This can be done most effectively by providing a certain quantity free, and establishing charges beyond that point. Another way is to automatically supply a certain quantity and request justification for additional quantities.

For existing literature with low stocks, delay reordering to see what effect being out of stock will have. If there is little or none, simply cancel the item.

CHAPTER 3

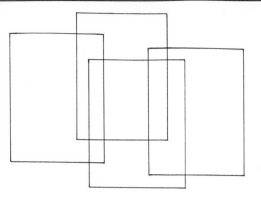

Testing for Overall Effectiveness

Effective communication requires two things: (1) a clearly defined objective for saying anything; and (2) a clearly defined understanding of who should listen and why. Without this knowledge most communications are bound to fail, and promotional literature is no exception.

For example, we all know that the media, style, and message appropriate to inform shareholders is different from that used to solicit customer orders. But if that knowledge is elementary, an extension of it is not. Very seldom are long-term investor concerns and company financial objectives considered in depth when preparing annual reports. And just as seldom are long-term marketing strategy and real customer needs considered when doing sales brochures.

The point is, effective promotional literature requires a complete understanding of a problem or opportunity from two viewpoints: that of the informer (seller) and that of the informee (buyer). How to make sure both are incorporated in the preparation of literature is the subject of Chapter 5.

Before considering that, however, it helps to have some benchmarks for judging performance; for considering what works best. Some tried-and-proven overall performance criteria are presented here. Chapter 4 covers 10 specific literature types and what usually works best in each.

THE WRITING MUST BE RIGHT

Never underestimate the interest of a reader. Like it or not, effective communications never takes place unless the writing is both interesting and suitable to the occasion.

Need proof? Consider food and sex. Even these elemental needs always benefit from the extra allure created by the written word. Surely, what you have to say is far less powerful.

Remember, too, that a style which will arrest one's attention and communicate in one situation, may not in another. Good literature writing always acknowledges the limitations and opportunities of the medium and considers and addresses the reader's latent interests. It then arrests and holds the reader's interests with a story that is both convincing and memorable.

THE VISUALS MUST TELL A STORY

To attract, hold, and persuade a reader usually takes more than words. At the very least, it involves the visual organization of words. More often, it requires a visual context and illustrations which enhance and extend the impact of the words. Whichever is the case, it is important to assure that the literature is visually complimentary to the story which should be told.

Sometimes literature succeeds best when it is visually dominant and driven; other times it succeeds when visuals merely support a written message. Knowing the right relationship between the two for the specific message to be conveyed—when to show and when to explain—is essential when considering whether the literature will work effectively.

THE CONTENT IS MOST IMPORTANT

Even good writing and strong visuals are not enough if the content, the *raison d'etre* of any literature, is not right. That's why assuring that the three conditions of the right content—completeness, accuracy and arrangement—are met is often the most difficult task in judging literature performance. And, to make matters even more difficult, content can be contained in the words, in the visuals, or in an equal mix of both.

After all, literate writing is not all that difficult; nor is arresting design. Creativity in both fields is fairly common. But add to that an additional need for intelligence, experience, and skill in gathering and distilling the material relevant to solving a communications problem, and you've got quite another situation entirely.

THE CRITERIA FOR JUDGING LITERATURE EFFECTIVENESS

Is the Literature Designed and Written for a Particular Task?
In general terms, the more specific and directed any literature is, the more effective it will be when used in the manner intended.

That is to say, for example, that product sheets oriented around specific applications facts will be more effective in most markets than those of a more general orientation. And that flyers will be most effective when used as a follow-up reminder soon after a major product introduction. But conversely, applications with specific facts will probably be inappropriate for a general audience. And flyers trying to function as product literature for a mature product will probably be a waste of money.

Of course, economics often dictate that literature be as general and multifunctional as possible; that it talk to many audiences, at different times, equally well. Nonetheless, to the extent possible, the various types of literature shouldn't be used in situations where they are not best suited.

Do You Like the Way the Literature Looks (Design) and the Way It Talks (Writing)?
Every good salesperson knows the importance of first impressions. And first impressions are formed by a combination of two things: appearance and articulation. If a salesperson doesn't look or sound right, the process of getting a potential customer to even pay attention to the content of the message becomes difficult; to persuade him or her to take the action desired becomes almost impossible.

So, too, with literature. If we think of literature as a printed means of persuasion, it should be evident that first impressions are every bit as important here as they are in personal selling.

Just what that first impression should be depends upon the overall message you wish to convey. But whatever it is, you should be able to pick up the literature piece and feel that it immediately conveys this message. Then, by just glancing at headlines and a few sentences of copy, you should also feel that it is organized and articulate in making this point.

Does the Literature Attract Interest, Encourage Readership?
In personal selling, after making a favorable first impression a good salesperson needs to hold the prospect's attention and to build interest in the product. The need is exactly the same in literature, but the process is different.

In personal selling, with face-to-face contact, the salesperson constantly judges the interest of the prospect and keeps adjusting and fine tuning the message to keep interest from flagging. In literature, however, there is no such on-scene ability. Decisions on what are the best ways to encourage interest (readership) must be made ahead of time, taking into account the varied interests of diverse readers.

If these decisions are well made, the literature will be visually appealing in a way that attracts and holds attention and makes reading easy. What is written must also be presented clearly, interestingly, and persuasively.

Does the Literature Offer Real Information and/or Benefits to the Reader? Continuing with the analogy, is your literature glib and vacuous, like a fast-talking pitchman? Or is the information selectively compiled and professionally related to the prospect's interests, as a professional sales representative would present it?

Because of literature's primary role of providing detail, and its place in the communications (sales) cycle, it is very important that what is produced have real content and show real benefits. If the opportunity is missed here, it may never come up again. Content is at least as important as style.

There are two questions to ask. First, is the literature written and designed to appeal to the reader's interests, rather than your interests? Second, is the information presented in a way that easily shows the benefits to the reader? Without exception, all good literature can pass these tests.

Is What Is Covered Important, and Is Everything Important Covered?   This is the test for completeness, so it varies with each type of literature, and with every idea or product presented. What is complete for a sales brochure describing a new product would not be complete for a capability brochure describing an organization.

Yet, each type of literature should have all the essential elements of a persuasive story, albeit with different degrees of detail. Remember, it is always better to have a few, well-organized words about many important things, than to have many words about only a few important things.

Making sure that only important points are selected from the abundance of information usually available involves considerable editing skill. And covering many important points well in a small amount of space tests the sophistication of preparation in combining words and graphics. Literature that covers all the essentials well, no more and no less, is good literature.

Can You Scan the Literature in a Minute or Less, Noting Only the Major Elements, and Get a Summary of the Whole Message?   If you can't, the literature isn't done well. The entire story should be understandable and persuasive to the reader who sees and reads *only* the major elements: headlines, lead-ins, subheads, graphics, photos, and captions. If the reader notes nothing more, and many won't, the literature must still be effective.

Of course, there would be no reason for multiple pages, long copy, and many graphics if they weren't useful. But their usefulness lies primarily in that they lend credibility and strength through the way they explain and expand the points made in the major elements. In addition, this explanatory material, which is primarily text, can provide the detail, facts, and specifications so necessary for the technical or careful reader.

When evaluating literature, always read it the way most readers do. First scan, then come back to read what is interesting. Never make the mistake of beginning at the beginning and ending at the end, as you would a novel. If you do, chances are that good literature will appear bad, and bad literature will appear good.

Does the Literature Lead You to Action, or a Conclusion? This is the bottom line. Is there an objective for the literature and has it been achieved?

Without exception, all literature should have a purpose, and that purpose should be some sort of response on the part of the reader. Perhaps the response is just feeling good about an organization. Or perhaps it is taking a customer one more step on the path to an eventual sale. Whatever the response, no literature is successful if the purpose for which it was prepared wasn't achieved. All literature is successful when its purpose is achieved.

There is one caveat: Success in meeting an objective says little or nothing about the efficiency with which it was accomplished. That judgment can come only from reviewing the literature in light of the other criteria.

SOME CAUTIONS ABOUT "AWARD-WINNING" LITERATURE

Evaluating the extent to which any given literature piece meets the criteria above is, of course, highly subjective. How do you determine whether a literature piece is truly first rate?

One way is to look for consensus. And it often comes from entering a literature piece in one or more of the various juried competitions sponsored by industry groups.

In addition, because of the subjectivity and uncertainty of any creative process, individuals involved in literature preparation need constant reinforcement. Popular mythology aside, it takes a truly exceptional artist to produce masterworks in a garret without the benefit of feedback and social interaction. Further, most commercial creativity is produced by teams of individuals, and it is hard to keep a team motivated if there is no outside recognition of the individual contributions of its members.

So it is that the various communications communities have instituted a number of competitions to consider, select, and publicize exceptional work. Most of these competitions are sponsored by a local advertising, public relations, or art directors' club and draw entries from the immediate geographic area. But some, such as the Andy Awards of the Advertising Club of New York, have national prominence. So, too, do awards presented by such national magazines as *Communications Arts,* which annually certifies the excellence of approximately 200 communications items—commercials, posters, packaging, literature, etc.—from over 21,000 submitted.

The positive aspect of awards is that they generally do everything they set out to do: they provide consensus; they give recognition where it is due; they promote the interchange of ideas and techniques; they produce fodder for discussion and criticism; and they provide a valuable social outlet. In short, they help raise the level of creative professionalism.

The other aspect of awards must also be recognized, however. There are several reasons why literature recognized for creative excellence might not be particularly effective *communications.*

First, many awards make a comment only on a particular type of artistry or craftsmanship. Design competitions recognize only graphic excellence, and copy competitions only writing excellence. Neither is necessarily related to total communications excellence. And even when total communications excellence is the major criterion, most competitions focus completely on creativity, and completely eschew marketing efficiency. There are a few exceptions, such as the Effie Awards given by the American Marketing Association, but they are noted for their uniqueness.

Put another way, what is creatively excellent should never be confused with what works best.* Ideally, they would always be one and the same, but, unfortunately, it doesn't seem to work that way.

Second, almost without exception, competitions reward most often that which is striking, cute, trendy, humorous, or otherwise unusual or different. Attracting attention is often equated with being good. Technique and emotion are often more highly valued

---

*Some twenty five years after the event, many advertising people still remember with embarrassment the case of the tire commercial that swept a series of creative competitions while actually managing to *reduce* sales, because of viewer brand confusion.

than substance. The better something looks, the better its chances, too. Existing materials, no matter how good, are usually not eligible. And tried and proven approaches, no matter how effective, are usually not rewarded.

Third, most competitions are inbred, and becoming more so, despite the best efforts of the sponsoring organizations to broaden the judging criteria. Most of those who judge the work actually do similar work. There are no professional critics with distance and objectivity, as there are in most other artistic fields. So there is a lot of creative masturbation and self-congratulation. The result is that, increasingly, creative effort goes into pleasing peers, not in creating that which works best. The opinions of professional critics may not necessarily always be right, but they come a lot closer than those of an artistic peer group, and they are a lot more useful in creating better performances.

Finally, and perhaps most significantly, literature is an also-ran category in most competitions, akin to a "best supporting canine actor" category at the Academy Awards. The major interest in most competitions is usually in broadcast commercials, followed by print ads, total communications programs, and everything else, including packaging and billboards.

In many competitions, literature is commonly lumped under the misnomer "collateral" and, with the exception of annual reports and a few high-visibility projects, is nearly always a low-interest category. Perhaps for this reason, there are seldom any judges with intimate knowledge of literature's uniqueness as a medium, its different formats, or what makes some pieces so much better than others.

In summary, don't automatically consider that literature that wins creative awards is necessarily the best. It is perfectly possible to have excellent literature and never win a creative award.

The best way to think of creative awards is as an important means to stimulate the individual and group morale that helps produce good work. Also recognize that literature that wins awards can provide good guidelines to what is current, stylish, and has creative impact. Most important, always make sure that your literature passes all the other criteria of effectiveness before considering it for any industry awards. If you do that, your literature will be truly first-rate regardless of whether or not it wins any creative awards.

CHAPTER 4

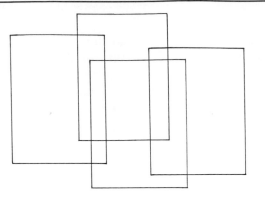

Ten Different Literature Types and What to Look for in Each

In this chapter, we group promotional literature into 10 common types and look at what makes each type unique. We also look at what works best within each type. This grouping is somewhat arbitrary, and is based on common physical appearance, common objectives, and common creative approaches.

This categorization is not intended to be all-inclusive, or even definitive. Rather, as in the case of the previous definition of promotional literature, it is intended only to provide some benchmarks; means around which a manager can organize literature strategy and judge the impact of individual pieces.

Annual Reports. This is the only type of literature many organizations are *required* to produce. All publicly traded companies must annually provide their shareholders with certain audited financial data and an accurate summary of company business.

This requirement, enforced by the threat of legal penalties

by the Securities and Exchange Commission, assures the annual report reader of both the importance and accuracy of what is printed. It also assures the company of a wide and influential audience. When properly handled, an annual report can be the single most productive medium a company has for positioning itself for future growth, regardless of whether it is big or small, prosperous or anemic.

For this reason, it is unique to annual reports that they usually suffer from too much attention and money, not too little. As what has been labeled "the great business art form," they attract the attention of the best financial, writing, and design talents in industry.

In looking at the yearly crop of annual reports, it is easy to wonder if the business of producing them hasn't become too large and inbred. Too often today's annual reports are glossy exercises in self-indulgence produced more to massage the egos of the sponsoring companies than to communicate vital concepts, ideas, and information to the outside world.

Financial World magazine, which for nearly 50 years has conducted a yearly competition to select the best annual reports, uses three criteria: (1) essential and appropriate information; (2) journalistic excellence; and (3) effectiveness of design. Not only do these three points sum up what is important, but the order is right as well.

To determine if your annual reports meet these criteria, look for the following: (See Appendix Four for more detail.)

- The cover should make a strongly positive statement about the organization—visually, in words, or both.
- Upon opening the report and leafing through it, the first impression should be that it was designed and written to be *read*. The second impression should be that the company is progressive and has a strong future ahead of it.
- The year's results should be graphically summarized in the beginning of the book in a way that compares them clearly with prior years' performance. The opening statement (Chairman's letter), should summarize events of the past year which have portent for the future, and present them in an easy-to-read form not more than two pages

long. There should also be a concise profile of the company's business.

- The editorial part of the report should be focused around the single theme—e.g., management strengths, productivity, operations—most appropriate to last year's results and next year's opportunities. Each editorial section should lead off with a statement that encourages readership, and be punctuated by helpful subheads. Illustrations and graphics should be coordinated with the text to make a concise, dramatic story.

- The financial data section should be clearly distinct from the editorial section. The financial tables should be typeset in a way that encourages reading.

- Quarterly reports should be considered as important as the annual report. They go to the same audience, so they should carry forward the same theme. Don't scrimp. In addition to quarterly facts and figures, use them to provide brief statements on what the company is doing that is of interest to shareholders and affects future profitability.

Capability Brochures.   These brochures profile a company, describing the organization and its abilities. The best ones are like an annual report without the financial data.

Capability brochures are particularly appropriate literature for suppliers of services, contractors, and organizations with diverse or unusually extensive facilities. That is, anywhere where it helps to show an organization's ability to deliver an unusual service, or perform on a commitment or promise.

For example, most businesses selling on a contracted price basis, such as government suppliers, find it necessary to convince the buyer of an ability to manage commitments—to maintain schedules and quality—as well as meet specifications and price. Similarly, sellers of services often need to reassure potential customers of their ability to deliver a nontangible product of high quality on time. And there is often a need for a company to explain what it does to groups as diverse as securities analysts and new employees.

Like an annual report, a good capability brochure must describe an organization. However, unlike an annual report, it isn't a luxury publication which is updated yearly. In addition, a capability brochure must go beyond reporting; it must also be persuasive. Unfortunately, there is usually much less time, money, and effort applied to capability brochures than annual reports.

While capability brochures come in all shapes, sizes and designs, the good ones are easy to spot. Chances are, they will have incorporated most of the following characteristics:

- An overall look, or feel, that is appropriately impressive—not terribly unusual and not ostentatious, but not common or cheap, either. Quality writing, design, photography and printing; because anything less reflects negatively on the sophistication of the organization.
- Size big enough to show seriousness and a story to tell, not so big as to overwhelm or confuse the reader (20 to 48 pages).
- A different strategy than that being used by competitors; one that builds or strengthens a unique position in the market. Coordination with other media to increase the brochure's usage and impact.
- A cover statement that captures the essence of the company and provides a rationale for picking up the brochure and reading to find out more. An extension and expansion of the cover message inside. Emphasis on what company elements—management, equipment, service—make it good to do business with.
- A logical organization of material presented to appeal to the reader's interests. A story completely summarized in major headlines, graphic elements, and photos. Adequate details for credibility in the text. An open, readable page layout.
- Avoidance of material that would date the brochure prematurely. Inclusion of material—offices, dealers, etc.—which allows the reader to follow up if desired.

Catalogs.   These can be powerful, persuasive tools, as all direct marketers can attest. Nonetheless, in many conventional marketing organizations the catalog is treated only as necessary overhead—specification material to be endured, rather than literature to be exploited. No literature displays greater variety or presents greater opportunity than the catalog.

In many industries catalogs are, at once, among the most common and most underutilized literature. A catalog is a recognized necessity for any organization providing an extensive, fragmented, or modular product line. It represents a regular and significant printing and distribution investment.

The catalog is usually welcomed by the recipient, too. Not to exploit this opportunity, not to consider every catalog as literature which can powerfully persuade as well as specify and inform, is to squander a valuable and expensive opportunity.

Although the purpose here is to consider what makes good literature, not the techniques of direct marketing, most of the same principles apply when it comes to catalogs. Good catalogs, whether for womens' clothing or machine tool parts, have the following characteristics in common:

- Catalog style and appearance have the family look of the organization's other printed material. There is continuity from issue to issue. If the organization issues several catalogs, each should have both individuality and a family appearance.
- The cover is distinctive and, where appropriate, highlights a few new products. If a large catalog, the cover carries a price to reduce waste and provide a sense of value. Large catalogs also have an easy-to-scan section index on the first facing page, perhaps keyed to tabs or graphic breaks throughout the book.
- The first section provides a brief summary of why the company is a good one to do business with—history, reliability, service, etc. Products are organized in sections that are easy for the reader to relate to his or her needs and interests. New products are highlighted in a separate "what's new" section, as well as fully described in regular text. There is a complete index at the end of the catalog if the number of entries warrants.
- An order form, complete ordering information, a list of dealers, and promotional text as a link to local dealers, is provided in a separate section.
- In the text, each item is summarized by a lead statement containing the major benefit or feature of the product. The text is as concise, descriptive, and interesting as pos-

sible. Every text block has similar form—interesting lead, descriptive paragraphs, specifications, order information, price.

* Illustrations are used whenever possible. All the illustrations have a similar look. Graphics are used occasionally to summarize and clarify differences between similar products.
* The design is sensitive to the way the catalog is distributed and used. The layout is open enough so that items and sections can be moved around in the future without necessitating extensive redesign.

Flyers and Broadsides (Handouts).   This literature type is best for a quick announcement or reminder. The faster, more dramatically this is accomplished, the more effective the publications are. They need provide no rationale, no persuasion, no detail. All they have to do is dramatically convey a short, direct, and powerful message.

Flyers and broadsides actually function as an advertising medium and are most effective when approached creatively from this perspective. They can be very effective at increasing local awareness, but will seldom motivate the reader to make anything more than an impulse decision.

Because they do function as an advertising medium, they usually work best when used intrusively, when they are passed out, stuffed in a mailbox, or put under the windshield wipers of cars in a parking lot. Therefore, both the cost of distribution and the effect on the recipient have to be carefully considered. The use of flyers or broadsides is very expensive on a cost-per-contact basis and, when not done well, their use can produce as many negative reactions as positive ones.

* This is not the domain of subtlety or subjective artistry. Directness and a strong sense of immediacy are important. The piece must not be cluttered with copy or graphics designed to provide style or rationale.
* If a single sheet is used, its purpose must be apparent at the first glance. If multiple pages are used, there must be a strong, compelling statement to encourage the reader to open it up.

- Copy and graphics must have impact and be easy to understand at a single glance. All copy and graphics must address one of four questions: (1) *what* is being offered; (2) *where* is it available; (3) *how much* does it cost; and (4) *why* take action now.
- The design objective should be to create immediate communication, even at the expense of good taste. Folds to provide a "reveal" work especially well. All design elements should be very strong, especially those associated with the name of the product and price.
- Copy orientation should be around the idea that less detail provides more impact; more detail provides less impact. There should be some reward offered for those who take immediate action.

Newsletters and House Magazines. These provide a unique means, complementary to other types of literature, of introducing new products, showing features, demonstrating expertise, and building loyalty. They can be among the strongest means available to influence a select group of individuals over an extended period of time.

At some point most organizations reach a size where it becomes important to communicate to employees, dealers, or customers on a regular basis. Newsletters and house organs provide this ability. While the form and appearance of the two types can be distinct, they are not radically different; newsletters are just more informal and less feature-oriented than house magazines.

Unfortunately, neither newsletters nor house magazines are usually thought of as literature, and therein lies a problem. To view them only as an independent form of corporate journalism leads to a greatly reduced impact. Further, they come to take on a life of their own and become unresponsive to any type of objective analysis. To avoid this, follow the guidelines below: (See Appendix Five for more detail.)

- The publication's purpose, and its fit with the organization's communications objectives, should be clearly and quantitatively defined. Who is the target audience? What activity or perception will the publication encourage?
- What is the appropriate frequency? What other publica-

tions will it be competing with for a reader's attention? How will circulation be attained?

- What is the procedure for continuous circulation updating? Is there a way to monitor progress against objectives? Is there a plan to kill the publication if objectives are not met after a reasonable time?
- Strategy should also be clearly defined. Is there an editorial plan? Does this plan mesh with and enhance the other communications activities of the organization? Is there enough information available on a regular basis to meet the plan? Is there sufficient staff to do a good job? Can the plan be accomplished on a realistic budget?
- A newsletter should contain mostly newsy items *of help or interest to the reader* (as opposed to your interest). A house magazine, should contain mostly feature articles which are both *interesting and informative to the reader* (as opposed to you).
- The publication's overall appearance should be complementary to both the image of the organization and its other printed materials. Graphic design should be strongly contemporary while encouraging interest and readership, especially if it is a new publication with no reputation to precede it. There should be strong design continuity from issue to issue.
- Numbering rather than dating individual issues reduces deadline pressure and encourages the reader to save past issues.
- The writing should be journalistic and professional—short and crisp for newsletters, long and with style for house magazines.
- Informative articles bylined by company personnel on their areas of expertise make strong features for house magazines. Product mention in such articles should be minimal; this is the place to impress the reader with knowledge, not the place for a sales pitch. In newsletters, items about the activities of people have most reader appeal.

Point-of-Purchase Literature.   There are two types: that used by a salesperson to help describe the product to the potential buyer, and that which attaches right to the product for the same purpose. In both cases, a concise summary of the benefits of purchasing is what's needed.

Literature for use by the salesperson can take several forms, one or more of which is appropriate to every sales organization. Perhaps the most common is the presentation (pitch) book, normally a loose-leaf binder with printed cards which provide summary points and illustrate and amplify a personal presentation. Other point-of-purchase literature includes items intended to remind and refresh the salesperson's memory before the sales call, such as feature or benefit summaries and objection or counter sheets.

The purpose of such literature is, simply, to make a salesperson's life easier and more productive. The more products handled, or the less experienced the salesperson is, the more critical the literature becomes. Providing this literature also assures that an organization's message is delivered more or less uniformly everywhere. This consideration is especially important when, for legal or marketing reasons, it is necessary to reach all potential customers with the same basic message at the same time.

Salesperson point-of-purchase literature should include these features:

- Presentation books should be designed to be easy to set up and flip through, graphically memorable, rugged enough for extended use, and readily customized for each call. They should contain: an introduction to the company and its product line; a two-line description of each product; half a dozen major features of each; pricing structure; a brief statement about the company's ability to deliver and service; an ordering summary; and a call for action.
- Indirect presentation literature (hidden prompters) should be designed for accessibility, compactness, quick scanning of important points, and fast reminder reading. They should contain: a summary of market needs; major product benefits; and counters to objections that may be raised.

Literature attached to the product being sold (usually a simple folder or sticker) provides the potential purchaser with reasons to select a product over others of a similar type. It is flattering to the intelligence of the potential buyer and also positions the product as one of superior quality which has hidden benefits requiring the need for additional explanation.

Direct point-of-purchase literature should include these features:

- It should take the form of a sticker or tag firmly affixed to the product in the most visible location. The product's major benefits should be bulleted. Easily examined, but otherwise obscure features should be pointed out.
- Construction strengths or material uniqueness should be highlighted. Any descriptive copy should assume a sale and be complimentary to the buyer ("Congratulations, you have just bought the finest. . ."). The company's reputation, or if unknown, its backup, should be mentioned.

Stuffers.   This is the most basic and least expensive type of quality product literature. Stuffers are small sheets or folders called that because they were originally used for stuffing into an envelope along with a monthly invoice. Now they enjoy much larger distribution because they can be produced in very large volume much less expensively than other literature.

Because they are small and inexpensive, many manufacturers provide dealers with well-produced, four-color stuffers at little or no cost. They usually have a space for local imprinting which allows the dealer to add price and ordering information. In other words, they provide the dealer with a way to obtain personalized, professionally produced literature at very low cost.

Stuffers are also perhaps the most versatile form of literature. Although often only thought of as manufacturer- supplied mailing enclosures for use by dealers, they also can be very effective for rack or counter use, as handouts, or anywhere a small literature piece will do the job. Because of their small size, however, there are several things to consider:

- Stuffers are ideal to use to stimulate demand for a new product. A single dramatic photograph can convey allure and romance. A scratch-and-sniff panel can allow thousands to sample a fragrance inexpensively. An enclosed fabric swatch can demonstrate quality.

- A stuffer with more than six or eight pages is hard to read and produces distracting bulk in such a small size.
- Small photographs and illustrations don't communicate as well, or provide the impact, of larger ones. Descriptive copy usually looks inappropriate, even if there is enough room (and usually there isn't). Use of dark colors will make stuffers more visible and less likely to get overlooked. But dark backgrounds also make text difficult to read.
- Company logo and product identification should be proportionately larger than in other literature to assure adequate impact. Product features are best summarized by a few bulleted statements. Any sentences should be simple and declarative. Design should be striking, and printing of high quality, to compensate for the small size.
- There should be adequate space for an imprinted dealer message, if appropriate. The imprint space should not be varnished.

Product Sheets.   Probably the most ubiquitous type of literature, these single sheets show and explain a product or service. It seems that everything involving a considered purchasing decision is covered by one. In most cases that's good, for an organization has both a need and an obligation to make information available on what it offers.

Product sheets are often called data, fact, detail, or spec sheets. And therein lies a tip-off to what the good ones contain. All well-produced product sheets share in common a sameness, an orientation around brevity, and a factual, objective style.

Product sheets are not the place for creativity. A formula, into which specific information can be plugged each time a new one has to be prepared, works much better and assures consistency. This is because a product sheet larger than six pages, or with expansive copy, or elegant design, has just too much going on to be really effective. In addition, product sheets should be used in as many ways as possible: as rack literature, as inserts to mailings, as package stuffers, as order forms, to answer requests for information, and so forth.

To assure that your product sheets are both well prepared and versatile, base the formula you use around the following:

- A strong visual identity of the company. A family resemblance to the company's other literature. Design consistency from sheet to sheet within a product line. An open layout that allows detail to vary in length from sheet to sheet without requiring design changes. 8½ by 11 inch size, universal-punched for notebook filing.
- The name of the product prominently placed. A dramatic photograph or illustration of the product. A brief two- to four-paragraph introductory description of what the product offers and to whom. A list of half a dozen, one-line product features. Several benefit headlines over copy blocks which briefly describe each of the major benefits of the product. A list of specifications necessary for initial consideration. A paragraph or two on service or backup support. Room for a dealer imprint.

Selling Brochures.   This is the next step up, everything a product sheet isn't and never should be. By way of contrast, selling brochures should be individualistic, expansive, and subjectively persuasive. This *is* the place for creativity. It is *not* the place for a formula approach.

This is also the bastion of the long-copy, dramatic-graphics, take-as-much-space-as-necessary, sell. In many instances, it is also the final opportunity available to persuade a potential customer to take positive action.

Of the 10 types of literature defined and covered here, selling brochures are, with the single exception of annual reports, normally the best thought out and most professionally produced. Like annual reports, and unlike most other literature, the importance of selling brochures in the sales cycle is well recognized. Room for improvement usually comes from resisting pressure to construct them either as an ad or a technical paper. To make sure neither happens, here are some tips:

- You have a story to tell—make it interesting. Involve the reader immediately and constantly. Rather than a mere label on the cover, provide a statement of intrigue, a benefit, or a challenge. Insist that the design be an important part of the message. Keep the writing lively and informative. Use dramatic photographs and illustrations.

- Construct the brochure like a good sales pitch by addressing the reader's needs in readily understandable terms. Summarize the problem or opportunity. Describe and show how your products address it. Add credibility by describing your company's experience and backup. Close by providing information on where to go, how to order.
- Break the brochure into several discrete, easily digestible sections. Start each section with a positive statement, or a question that piques the reader's interest. Pay off the section headlines with subheads that summarize benefits or provide answers.
- Keep sentences and paragraphs short, but varied. Use photography and illustrations aimed at capturing the interest of the reader rather than merely showing the product. Avoid heavy pages.

Instruction Books.   These are a good test for communications sophistication. Ask anyone about their role in the communications mix. If the answer is that they are never read, therefore there's no need to spend much money on them; he or she flunks. So does anyone who believes that yes, they are read, but they must be pedantic to be effective.

Instruction books are both an obligation and an opportunity. Unfortunately, they are too often thought of only in the former context. The obligation is to help a customer who has just done the courtesy of purchasing your product to use it well. This presents you with the opportunity to win the customer's loyalty, enthusiastic recommendation, and future sales.

Because instruction books come with the product, it should never be forgotten that, like it or not, every instruction book (including documentation supplied with software) will do one of two things: (1) it will *reinforce* the negative or positive impressions of the buyer; or (2) it will *overcome* the negative or positive impressions of the buyer. To make sure that your instruction books always reinforce the positives and overcome the negatives, look for these features:

- The cover should convey sophistication, friendliness, and ease of use. There should be no confusion as to what the product is, or who makes it. Avoid cover labels like "instruction manual"; much better is a positive statement like "tips to help you enjoy . . ." If the size of the product packaging permits, make the book large enough to be easily held and read. If appropriate, provide more than one book to make communications easier.

- Consider where the book will be stored and used. Make sure the format is appropriate for use under these conditions. Make sure the book can be read under these conditions.
- Start the book with a friendly, informal statement about the product, the company, and how the customer is welcomed into the family of users. Keep the design open, airy, and inviting.
- Break the book into half a dozen or so thumb-indexed sections. Provide a quick "where to turn to" index first thing. Use sequencing—(1), (2), (3), and so on—wherever appropriate. Use illustrations to make as many points as possible. Use color breaks or other techniques to clearly differentiate different subjects.
- Line drawings are often clearer than photographs. Spots of color can focus emphasis. Avoid color photographs unless the color helps explain. Use very brief, declarative sentences.
- Provide tips and suggestions as well as instructions. Don't be afraid to mention things to avoid—it enhances credibility. Include a troubleshooting section. Show how to get help fast: include customer service locations or toll-free telephone numbers. Give necessary specifications. Enclose the product warranty.
- For very sophisticated products, consider whether a videocassette can be useful in providing more information or replacing many of the traditional functions of a printed instruction book.

CHAPTER 5

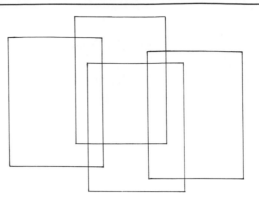

Managing Literature Preparation

Previous chapters have shown literature's importance in promotional communications, defined the medium, set need and budget criteria, and provided tests for judging performance. These preliminary steps are necessary before one can lay the foundation for the larger subject of how to produce effective literature most efficiently.

Literature preparation is very much a people business, which makes it highly creative and unstructured. Exactly the same problem, presented to two individuals at the same time will always result in two distinct solutions. The overall concept, graphic design, illustrations, and writing style will be quite different. In short, *what* is communicated, as well as the *way* in which the communication takes place, will depend on the unique approach of the individual problem solver.

Depending upon your viewpoint, this can make literature preparation creative and exciting. Or, it can make it very frustrating, especially if you feel uncomfortable with anything that cannot be precisely specified and defined. To help increase the excitement and minimize the frustration, it is important to know exactly who does what and what options are available. Only with this background will it be possible to establish the procedures that can effectively tap creative energy and build productive working relationships.

WHO DOES WHAT

Regardless of literature type, sophistication, or expense, there are five separate and distinct areas of activity involved in its preparation. Each area can involve one or more specific job functions.

Although it is certainly possible for one individual to handle functions in two or more of these areas (project management and writing, for example), this is usually *not* the way to get the best results, for each of the five involve often conflicting disciplines. Additionally, the creation of separate but dependent areas of responsibility provides an effective check and balance against excesses. And it generates the need for cooperation and interaction which always acts as a stimulus to better work.

Project Management. Mao Tse-tung said that political power comes from the end of a gun. The organizational analog to that truism is that business power comes from a budget. Since project management is where the budget for literature preparation resides, this alone makes it first among otherwise equal activities. It is another truism that *more bad literature comes from bad project management than from any other cause.*

The management of literature projects is seldom the sole responsibility of an individual. Most often, it is one of several communication responsibilities (ad manager), one of several marketing responsibilities (product manager), or one of several very diverse responsibilities (president). Whatever the case, the project manager's role is nothing less than to get effective literature produced on time and on budget, much the same as a producer does for a motion picture, or a publisher does for a magazine.

To do this, especially in conjunction with other responsibilities, takes a certain amount of directed energy. Perhaps more important, it also takes a degree of objectivity that is difficult to maintain for anyone actively involved in other preparation activities.

The project manager's role, then, should not be to do any of the work. Rather, it should be to set objectives, establish a budget, select a creative team, approve their efforts, and be responsible for the results.

The ideal person for this responsibility should have a rare balance of the two, often antithetical, fundamental approaches to life. This individual should be able to work well in the objective world of specifics: numbers, budgets, and analyses. And, in addition, relate equally well to the subjective world of concepts: ideas, feelings, and impressions. While such a rare talent is inbred, it can often be identified in individuals who have both past creative experience, and a strong ambition to organize and control the events of the future.

Writing.   Every literate person can write, and therein lies a problem: For not every literate person can write well. Furthermore, even persons who write well often write promotional literature poorly. Writing well is a talent; writing literature well is a talent enhanced by craftsmanship. The latter is too seldom seen.

Writers of much of today's literature are of two types. The first is the individual who is normally responsible for other tasks but who is pressed into service to write an occasional brochure or data sheet. The second type is the copywriter who normally writes ads or direct mail solicitations and who is asked to crank out a literature piece. The signatures of both are usually apparent.

In the case of the individual doing the occasional piece, the writing is usually marked by a lack of selectivity, a confusion in organization, and a pedantic style. In the case of the copywriter, the copy is often too aggressive, too cute, and much too brief to convey the appropriate message.

In contrast, a good writer of literature knows how to select and compile information and develop a concise, persuasive story from it in a prescribed amount of space. The writer is not deterred by the necessity of undertaking a relatively lengthy project of research, organization, and writing. Nor is the writer mired in the fashions of most copywriting, which are borne from the inappropriate (in this situation) need to quickly get the reader's attention, make just one or two strong points, and rely upon the cumulative effect of future viewings for memorability.

A good writer of literature is someone with a flair for words, personal selling experience, and a strong sense of what comprises a logical, persuasive argument. Although he is a kind of copywriter, the writer of literature is also as different from most other copywriters as a print reporter from a TV reporter. What such a writer produces has appropriate content enhanced by a creative execution and applied to a well-defined purpose. For a complete discussion of what comprises good literature writing, see Chapter 9.

Designing. Since many fewer individuals claim to have artistic than writing talent, and even fewer have any formal training, literature design is nearly always left to professionals. Perhaps because of this, a specific type of artistic discipline—graphic design—has grown along with the importance of persuasive communications in our society.

Graphic designers are highly trained and specifically skilled individuals. Their job is to apply aesthetic principles and artistic talents to the solving of the visual problems associated with any type of graphic communications.

This means that unlike the writing, which may be unpredictably excellent or terrible, literature design usually meets at least minimal aesthetic standards. It is, for example, rare to see a well-written and poorly designed piece, while it is common to see one that's well designed and poorly written.

But not all professionally designed literature is as good as it should be. Training alone is hardly a guarantee of good taste or effectiveness. Moreover, there are several occupational hazards which afflict all graphic designers from time to time.

The first occupational hazard is an inability to communicate the right message because of a lack of understanding of the product or service being offered. Sometimes what appears at first to be an aesthetically pleasing design is later found not to work well because it puts emphasis in the wrong places.

A second hazard is creative overkill. All designers want to do the best job possible. But under the pressure of trying to do this, sometimes the best becomes easily confused with the largest, the most expensive, the most demanding, or the most artistically satisfying.

A third hazard is designing for other professionals, not for the real, less-sophisticated world. Literature design can never be too good, provided that good is defined as that which works best. Unfortunately, sometimes designers who talk primarily to other designers define good as that which has the strongest peer approval.

The final occupational hazard is trendiness. All design, from housing to fashion to literature, responds to trends. And rightly so, for readers relate and respond better to that which appears to be current and fashionable. But trends come and go, and nothing is less effective today than what was *au courant* a year ago. Good design takes advantage of trends that can be used effectively and avoids those which cannot, regardless of their popularity.

The fact that the effect of many of these hazards can be seen every day in all kinds of literature, indicates only that designers are no better than other professionals in being objective about their own work. Far more significant, however, is that individuals responsible for approving literature too often fail to exercise their veto prerogatives over inappropriate design. For more specific information on how to evaluate literature design, see Chapter 10.

Approving.   All literature should undergo two types of approval. The first, which assures adherence to internal concerns such as strategy and tactics, checks to see that everything that should be covered has been covered, and in the best way. The second, which assures compliance with external concerns such as legal and other obligations, checks to make sure that what must (or must not) be said hasn't been overlooked.

The approval review process can involve as many individuals as appropriate, given the size of the organization, the complexity of the idea, and its importance to the future. In general, however, it is in every organization's interest to have as few individuals as possible involved, and to get their comments as early as possible.

Only one approval review cycle should be planned, and it

should begin as soon as all copy, design, and illustration elements are available. Providing only one opportunity to comment on the literature not only conserves the valuable time of the reviewers, but also forces a certain amount of reviewing discipline. Conducting the approval review early, while still at the typewritten copy and layout sketch stage, allows changes to be made much less expensively than if done after type has been set and pages constructed.

Include in the approval for *internal* concerns only a few individuals with a need to know, or a need to check accuracy. Limiting the number of reviewers always results in better, more focused literature. This is because, when asked to review a document, most people will feel an obligation to criticize, suggest, and change. When more than 10 individuals are included in this process, the literature often ends up with a confusion of ideas and styles.

If policies require more than 10 reviewers, one way to be accommodating without affecting quality is to separate routings into *approval, information only,* and *fact checking* segments.

The degree to which *external* concerns are addressed by approval routing depends largely on the type of business the organization is involved in and its history of regulation, compliance, and litigation. While it is generally true that small organizations have less reason for concern than large organizations, one of the things that allows an organization to become large and powerful is its attention to such details.

In large organizations, routing should include the corporate legal staff; in small organizations it should include an outside legal counsel skilled in communications procedures, precedents, and practice. In either case, the role should not usually be one of legal approval—the making of hard and fast judgments about what to say or do. Rather, it should be one of legal advice— pointing out the relative dangers of using certain words, phrases, or illustrations, or of taking certain courses of action.

Legal routing should look for the following: less than complete or truthful descriptions of products and ideas; misleading impressions a reader might get from the words or illustrations; the availability of substantiation for any claims made; that sources of any factual statements are identified; that all company tradenames and trademarks are identified and used properly. For tips and techniques which will make approval routing easier, see Appendix One.

Producing.   This is the activity of physically making the printed literature after all the creative work has been completed and approved. It primarily involves printing; but sometimes typesetting, mechanical (page) preparation, and other functions are included, although more often they are included in the design process.

No matter how all-inclusive the production process is, chances are it will consume the bulk of most literature budgets. Production expenses run from 50 percent to 90 percent of the cost of most literature; longer runs and larger pieces result in a higher percentage of the cost, shorter runs and smaller pieces incur a lower percentage of the cost. In addition, production usually accounts for the longest segment of the total time from the literature's conception to its distribution.

Production can be handled in several different ways, depending upon the organization and its resources. Organizations which produce a large volume of literature often employ production professionals who have training and experience in the printing industry. Their job is to specify services, obtain estimates, contract to buy, assure quality control, arrange for distribution, and provide payment.

Small and middle-sized organizations most often rely upon the designer of the literature for production. This can involve responsibility for all production functions, or an á la carte working arrangement where the designer handles only a few functions—for example, quality control, but not the obtaining of estimates or the payment for services, which are handled directly by the organization.

In addition, some organizations prefer to rely upon the reputation of their suppliers to assure that things are done cost-effectively and well. When one considers the number of subjective judgments involved and the obvious conflict of interests, this method can hardly be recommended. But it must be noted that many organizations with long-standing supplier relationships will have it no other way.

Whichever production method is used, the process is both complex and full of pitfalls for the unwary. Therefore, it is wise to keep in mind the two constants of good production management: (1) never agree to anything unless you understand exactly what is going to happen, when it will take place, and how much it will cost; (2) the sooner you change something, the less expensive the change will be. For information that will help you more clearly understand the production process see Chapter 11.

THE IMPORTANCE OF THE CREATIVE TEAM

The next chapter covers the options available in getting literature produced. Before getting into that, however, it is important that a manager realize the importance of the actual creative team that will do the work.

Each of the five functions described above is usually handled independently of the others with the exception of the two creative functions, writing and design. Normally, they should be a team effort. This is because communication via printed literature involves the need for complementary visual and written creativity. In contrast, the other functions involve steps that are uncomplementary; they provide a check and balance for each other.

Some literature succeeds best when visually dominant and driven, some when visuals merely support a written message. Knowing the right relationship between the two—when to show and when to explain—is essential to effectiveness. That comes intuitively to a good creative team.

In addition, a team effort helps avoid the trap of excessive creativity. A skilled writer and designer team, working together, provides a much more objective and balanced approach than individuals working alone. This team effort provides strong, cost-effective literature, as opposed to a "neat solution" to some perceived problem.

It is surprising how much literature is first written then turned over to a designer for layout, or how many designs are created with space to be later filled with words. Such practices not only run the strong risk of mediocre creativity, but they add unnecessary expense as well.

The writer and designer team need not work together all the time, or even for the same organization. Indeed, the individuals involved will probably be stronger creatively if they work with a variety of other people on different projects. They need only have similar availability, personalities, working habits, and creative approaches.

If you ask an organization such as a design firm to prepare your literature, they will choose the creative team. If you opt to work with in-house or free-lance staff, pick either a writer or designer whose work you are familiar with and ask him or her to pick a team member.

Before making a commitment, however, look at samples of work they have done together and make sure you like what you see and read. Also, make sure that both team members— not just the writer—understand your business and will learn about the product. Finally, make sure one individual has overall responsibility for the team's performance.

TEN WAYS TO BE A BETTER PROJECT MANAGER OR CLIENT

1. Before the first meeting with the creative team, define your needs exactly. Set precise objectives and a time-table.
2. At the first meeting, be as organized and detailed as possible. Provide complete facts and full backup information.
3. Give the creative team enough time to do research, develop an idea, and prepare a concept—at least one week, maybe two—before they present the concept.
4. Don't be afraid to demand great work. But make sure you can recognize it when you see it.
5. When reviewing creative work, try to visualize what the piece will look like when printed. Check the overall impression, scan the headlines and illustrations, then read the text quickly.
6. Don't nitpick over details or style. Everyone has idiosyncrasies. Yours will be different from those of the readers anyway.
7. When suggesting changes, state as precisely as possible what is wrong. Don't tell how to fix it.

8. Be consistent in your comments and criticisms.
9. Let the creative team know you appreciate the effort they have put into your literature.
10. Be sure all suppliers—creative team, printers, and so on—make money. It will do more than anything else to guarantee future loyalty and good work.

CHAPTER 6

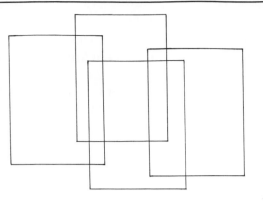

In-House versus Out-of-House Preparation

Should any or all of the literature preparation functions described in Chapter 5 be handled by an in-house staff? Or will better results or lower costs come from hiring outsiders to do the work? If so, which outsiders?

This elementary, "make inside or buy outside?" question has been around for as long as man has put pen to paper for persuasive purposes. And there is no better answer now than before because organizations and situations still differ widely. But there are more options now, and there are some trends worth pondering.

In general, consumer-oriented organizations, with fewer products that have fewer real differences from those of competitors, are more likely to go outside to find the creativity their literature needs to be noticed. Industrial and business-to-business organizations, with many complex products requiring detailed knowledge to describe, are likely to use inside staff in an effort to obtain accuracy and economy.

It is the author's experience that about half of all promotional literature is currently prepared by in-house staff, and about half is prepared by outside vendors. This compares to about 60 percent done in-house a decade ago. There are many reasons for the shift. The often hidden high cost of internal staff and the need for more creatively stimulating literature in increasingly competitive worldwide markets are two important reasons. It will be a long time, however, before outside preparation is right for many organizations.

Anyone who has ever tried to purchase creative or production services can attest that the individuals and firms offering them, internally and externally, can always provide detailed reasons why they can do a particular job better than anyone else. Because for many managers the production of literature is an occasional job to be squeezed in along with many others, it is particularly difficult to take the time to objectively view the various available options.

Therefore, to provide balance, what is presented here is the *other* side of the story—the limitations of each of the various literature preparation alternatives that are available.

YOUR LITERATURE PREPARATION ALTERNATIVES

In-House Staff.   That there are fewer individuals now engaged in preparing literature in-house than in the past is partly a function of the ever-increasing cost of employee benefits and the resulting pressure in organizations to buy more routine services outside. It is also partly due to the general trend in industry towards decentralization and less vertical integration as a way of shaving costs. And, finally, it is partly due to the continuing evolution towards the increased specialization of industry.

The economic arguments for or against an in-house staff are obviously very organization specific. They usually revolve around the actual, as opposed to apparent, cost of personnel and overhead, and the real level of productivity. Unfortunately, the larger question of the quality of in-house work and its effectiveness, is seldom as thoroughly examined. It should be. These are some limitations of in-house staff:

- It is hard to attract the best creative individuals to work in a large, noncreative organization because they often feel out of place and constrained by its highly structured environment.

- With only a weekly pay check as an incentive, it is difficult for a creative individual to be as motivated to extraordinary effort as if his or her pay were directly related to performance.
- Individuals have much less exposure to a variety of creative ideas and approaches when most of their work tends to be for the same products and markets.
- Staff size, experience, and talent may limit what can be accomplished in-house, and how fast.
- Policies may limit the freedom to replace unproductive individuals, or even require their utilization on certain types of work.
- The work often lacks objectivity because it is both prepared and approved by the same organization that will use it.

Free Lances.   It is the dream of most writers and designers to one day stop working for someone else and go into business as a free lance—in other words, to do their own thing on their own schedule without splitting the income from their creativity with anyone else.

The capital needed and the overhead assumed are low: a telephone, some letterhead stationery, and a desk, probably at home. The risk is low, too, because if the free-lance business doesn't work out, another job can probably be found easily; creative opportunities are based on talent, not on organizational seniority. For these reasons, a large number of writers and designers try the free-lance route every year.

For the organization looking for either highly creative talent or below average prices, these individuals present an underutilized resource. But there are caveats: Free lances are also a diverse and volatile group. Some limitations of free lances are:

- The free lances you employ today may not be available or in business, tomorrow.
- There are usually no performance guarantees. You buy an individual's time and are expected to pay for it regardless of satisfaction. So select carefully.

- Don't assume that any free lance can undertake any literature assignment. For example, many journalists have the wrong discipline for writing literature. And some designers specialize in a certain type of design and aren't very good at other types. Ask to see samples of earlier work that's similar to what you have in mind.
- The free lance may not have the resources to get the whole job done. Or get it done on time. Be specific about what is expected, and when.
- If you are hiring two free lances to work together as a team, make sure they have worked together before, or that they are at least compatible in style and world view.
- Make sure that the free lance is excited about doing your literature, and doesn't simply view it as a way to cover expenses while working on "The Great American Novel," or "Great Art."

Public Relations Agencies. Broadly defined, public relations is the activity of supplying positive information about an organization in a timely manner. The best way to do this is through the news media, but there are times when only literature can do the job well, or when it is needed to further amplify or explain.

All public relations agencies handle literature, and most are particularly well versed in preparing those types which convey information: annual reports, newsletters, and house organs. In all cases, however, literature is only a minor part of what a public relations agency does, so be aware of what this means in terms of the ability to produce good work, on time and on budget. Be aware of these limitations of public relations agencies:

- Most agencies work on a retainer, rather than a project, basis. They may be reluctant to accept a literature assignment without a larger commitment.
- Many agencies are small operations with limited resources. If they simply farm out your literature to free lances, you get nothing more than you can purchase yourself, usually cheaper.
- Some agencies specialize in a certain activity, such as press relations, financial relations, or sports contacts. Don't let them to do your literature unless you have similar interests.

- Many public relations personnel have strong communications skills, but little or no experience in marketing, or any of the skills of persuasion.
- Writers in a public relations agency tend to have mostly journalistic experience, not copywriting experience. What they write is often descriptive, but dull.
- Only the largest public relations agencies have designers on staff, and those that do don't attract the best talent. Whether farmed out or done internally, the result is often mediocre work.
- The priorities of all public relations agencies revolve around daily news events. Other activities—such as literature— tend to get less attention and be assigned to "the second team."

Sales Promotion Agencies.   Sales promotion agencies (sometimes called marketing services agencies) evolved from the specialized groups within many large advertising agencies which handled nonmedia activity. This activity includes literature, but it also includes the potentially more lucrative and exciting business of conceiving, creating, and running promotions which stimulate product sales through special deals, price reductions, couponing, and tie-ins.

Since literature preparation involves a wholly different set of disciplines and skills from promotion, it has become increasingly difficult for one organization to do both well in today's highly specialized and competitive agency environments. For this reason, most large sales promotion agencies now specialize in promotions, a few specialize in literature, and some still claim to handle both equally well. These are some limitations of sales promotion agencies:

- If the agency solicits both literature and promotion work, ask for examples of literature preparation time and cost, as well as samples.
- Many agencies are consumer product oriented. If yours is not a consumer product need, make sure the agency can understand your business before giving it an assignment.
- The agency may not have the staff, enthusiasm, or experi-

ence to handle literature. Still, many will accept such an assignment. Don't assume willingness to be the equivalent of ability.

- After years of doing highly specialized work, some agencies develop business methods and a style that may be inappropriate for your literature. Ask for samples and discuss working arrangements.
- The agency overhead may be high, resulting in high costs.
- Many agencies specialize in certain industries, such as travel. In choosing an agency, make sure it has experience in your business as well.
- Many agencies produce literature to a formula for a set price. Don't expect creativity or quality under these circumstances.

Advertising Agencies. Today, most advertising agencies promote themselves as full-service organizations. In other words, they provide total communications support for their clients. In such cases, it is natural for an organization to ask its agency to also prepare its literature.

Unfortunately, the history and disciplines of advertising make it difficult for an agency to perform this function well, unless the literature is tied directly to an advertising campaign. As a recognition of this limitation, but also as a recognition of another profit opportunity, many agencies have lately taken to forming separate, semiautonomous departments to separate literature preparation from their other advertising functions.

The fact that these departments are often referred to as the "collateral group," or that they are made part of the public relations or design staffs, indicates that most agencies still have a long way to go before they eliminate their discrimination against literature. These are some limitations of advertising agencies:

- All large agencies and many small agencies work on a total service, rather than a project, basis. They will only accept a literature assignment as part of a total package of advertising services.
- Even the very largest agencies often do little literature work. They may have less actual literature experience than a small design firm or individual free lances.

- Very few agency writers and designers think of literature as a stimulating assignment. By training and aspiration most want to work on TV commercials and large print campaigns.
- Very few agency account executives have any interest in managing the preparation of literature. Most consider it an aspect of client service to be endured.
- Advertising style and techniques of arresting attention, communicating quickly, providing memorability, and doing it over again and again, invariably and inappropriately creep into literature.
- Most agencies have the "collateral" mind set. Don't let such an agency prepare your literature unless collateral (that is, material tied to your advertising) is what you are actually interested in.
- Agency accounting methods—especially in those agencies where most income is from media commissions—tend to make literature preparation and production very expensive.

Design Firms.   The most visually striking and appealing literature usually comes from design firms. Because these firms bring a group of graphic designers together in one location, the result is a high degree of creative stimulation, criticism, and perfection. Sometimes this is what works best for literature, and sometimes it is not.

The major asset as well as limitation of a design firm is its single focus. Other organizations that prepare literature tend to employ individuals with diverse training, backgrounds, and interests. Most of the people in a design firm are of a single, visual, mind-set. This can result in the direction, intensity, and perseverance necessary to get superior literature. But it can also result in the ignorance, inflexibility, and arrogance which can make even the best-looking literature an inappropriate disaster. These are some other limitations of design firms:

- Some graphic design firms are more interested in such projects as packaging, corporate identity, and signage than literature. Ask to see samples of recent literature projects.

- Some firms are more interested in producing art than communications. A sure giveaway is a willingness to produce
layouts without even a copy outline.
- There is a tendency in some firms to approach a project
from a purely visual, rather than a business strategy viewpoint. Try to determine their level of business sophistication.
- Few firms have writers on their staff. If the client doesn't
supply the writing, they will contract it out to free-lances
and provide it at a high markup.
- In larger firms the actual graphic designer on the project
may be discouraged from meeting with the client. Yet,
the best results often come when the designer can experience, firsthand, the client's problems and opportunities.
- It is hard for any design firm to bring itself to do minimal
design, even when it is the most effective form of communication.
- All design firms develop a certain look and style. Be comfortable with that style before making any assignments.
- Some very creative design firms are very poorly run businesses. Insist on proper financial accounting and regular
progress reports to minimize cost overruns and any other
surprises. Ask for client references.

KEEPING COSTS IN LINE

To write at length here about actual, or even relative, costs for
literature preparation would commit these words to nearly immediate obsolescence. Better instead to just touch upon billing procedures, expectations, and ways to control costs.

Printing fees for literature are nearly always quoted on a
firm-price basis, with payment upon satisfactory delivery. The
usual procedure of obtaining three competitive bids should be
followed as described in Chapter 11. Otherwise, purchasing is
a complex subject, and further elaboration is beyond the scope
of this text.

On the other hand, determining payment for writing and design is far less standardized. Billing can be either for time ex-
pended, or a quoted price, and is usually on a best-effort basis.
The reason for the best-effort basis is simply the subjective na-

ture of creative work. The writer or designer could, theoretically, spend an infinite amount of time making changes to suit personal idiosyncrasies.

Many writers and designers only accept work for which they can bill on a time-expended basis. In this arrangement, a minimum and maximum fee is usually specified and an hourly or daily fee agreed upon. The final cost of the assignment depends on the time it takes to complete the work. If the work reaches the maximum time specified, it stops until a new arrangement is agreed upon.

While this arrangement may sound a bit one-sided, with proper controls it can work to the benefit of both parties. For the creative person it eliminates most of the pressure to cut corners to maximize profit that results from fixed-price quotes. For the organization buying the creativity, providing detailed source material and organizing fewer meetings that are better planned can directly result in a lower bill. If a detailed estimate of costs is provided, and if it is supplemented with scheduled progress reports, there will be few opportunities for surprises or fraud.

CHAPTER 7

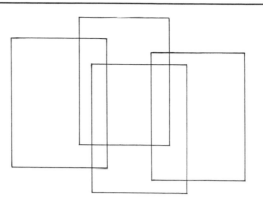

Examples of How Several Organizations Use Literature to Save Money

The best way to think of your organization's promotional literature is as a group of surrogate employees, silently dispensing information and impressions. As with any group of employees, a good manager will assign certain literature types to work in the areas for which they are best suited, matching personality to the specific job.

Doing this well will probably lower the cost of doing business because a good literature program will save far more in labor and media expenditures than it costs.

In this chapter we will look at 14 short case histories which show how a variety of organizations have successfully used literature to make their communications and marketing programs less costly. The examples show a breadth of products, markets, and ideas. The criteria for selection were innovation and savings, not necessarily the creativity of presentation. Also note that there isn't necessarily any correlation between how well each piece works and how much it cost to produce. What's important is the net effect—its efficiency to the organization.

Organization: Polaroid Corporation.
Product: Identification Systems.
Literature type: 8-page sales brochure/2-page data sheets.
Use: Sent in response to inquiries; sales call leave-behind.

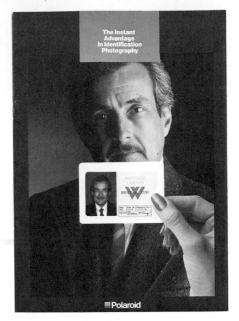

Brochure cover

Representative inside spread

Often a company has specific products which share many features with others in a line. Should several small brochures be produced, each of which tells the company story and describes a single product? Or should one large brochure be produced which tells the company story once and provides specifics on all of the individual products? The first option produces expensive literature redundancy. The second option produces the added expense of providing heftier literature than most customers need, or want to read.

The above example avoids that dilemma. A relatively small, 8-page brochure with a back pocket tells the general company story. Individual, 2-page data sheets custom-inserted into each brochure according to the customer's interests provide the product specifics.

The brochure's cover encourages the reader to open it and discover that "the instant advantage" is the ability to go from a sitting to a finished photo ID card quickly. Inside pages establish that Polaroid ID systems are always state-of-the-art, and show applications and variety. The individual data sheets, custom-inserted into the back cover pocket, show product and use and provide a listing of important specifications.

Data sheet front   Data sheet back

Organization: W. Atlee Burpee.
Products: Garden Tools.
Literature type: 4-page flyer.
Use: Counter pass-out.

Front cover   Back cover

Counter use of literature can be a good way to get information to a selected audience and to produce incremental, impulse sales. But shoppers are usually in a hurry. So, to work, counter literature must be direct and very interesting—much like an ad. This piece is a good example of how well-applied creativity can make that happen.

The front cover immediately establishes the name of the company,

Inside spread

shows the product, and creates an *event*. If you were in a garden store and interested in tools, this would be tough to pass up. The back cover makes an offer you can't refuse and provides a place for a dealer stamp or imprint. Inside the flyer, the company's line of tools, and what makes them different and better, is explained and shown in a fashion that encourages fast reading yet has lasting impact.

Organization:	Paine Webber Incorporated.
Product:	Real Estate Limited Partnership.
Literature type:	24-page sales brochure.
Use:	Account executive pass-out.

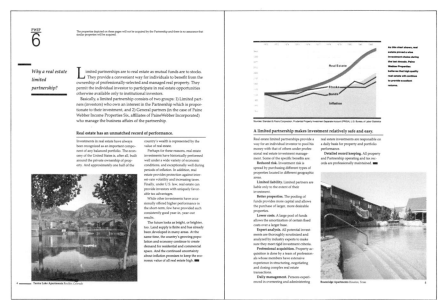

Cover

Courtesy of Paine Webber Inc.

Representative inside spread

Most of us treat investment opportunities with considerable skepticism, and that's often the way we treat an account executive's recommendation. We want to make up our own minds, based on the facts.

The financial sales literature we are usually given seems designed to obfuscate and does little to allay our wariness. Why isn't it possible to have the deal explained, the risks shown, and the potential reward indicated in a simple, interesting, and informative way?

Well, it is. This sales literature is clear, concise and just detailed enough; it provides explanation without condescension. It will shorten the time needed to close the sale because it provides the reassurance we all need—that we'll be in good hands if we invest with Paine Webber.

Organization:	General Electric Company.
Product:	Telephones.
Literature type:	24-page point-of-purchase booklet.
Use:	Counter distribution.

Cover

Easy installation.
General Electric Telephones and accessories utilize the modular plug and jack system. If you already have modular jacks in your home, installation is as easy as plugging in an appliance. Or, it's a breeze to convert to modular jacks using GE accessories and this booklet. (Pages 19-23.)

Electronic Technology Solves Your Telephone Problems
General Electric Telephones are designed to offer you new exciting telephone benefits. All with the quality and durability you expect. For instance, GE's 2-9350 Speaker phone allows you to talk and wander around the room without holding the phone. Go about what you're doing and talk on the phone at the same time. Or, if remembering telephone numbers is a nuisance, there's the 2-9260 Hotline. It remembers 9 frequently called numbers plus 3 Emergency Numbers. If busy numbers are a problem, try GE's 2-9260 memory dialer. It automatically redials busy numbers and calls you back with a different sounding ring, when the line is open.

Use this booklet to help find the model that's right for you.

How to Shop

The most significant thing you need to know about buying a telephone is . . . "All phones are not created equal!" There are significant differences leading to wide price variations.

QUALITY is the most important thing to look for in any telephone. Remember that a phone is not a luxury . . . it's a necessity.

RELIABILITY. It must work when needed. Many phones are designed to work well under optimum conditions. But, phone networks vary, and don't always give these optimum conditions — your phone should work every time, regardless of the network conditions.

DURABILITY. A phone must withstand the rigors of everyday use. It is dropped, exposed to moisture, lightning surges, tugging, pulling and more. Does the phone offer:

- Sealed, polymer cone speaker elements
- Rugged ABS plastic construction
- Top quality electronic components
- Lightning surge protection
- Keys with numbers that won't rub off
- Consumer replaceable cords
- Stainless steel antennas (on cordless)
- Corrosion resistant keypad contacts

CONVENIENCE. Today's new phones often cut corners. Some things to look for:

- Automatic Hook Switch (A phone should be "on" when you pick it up. Beware of "off/on" switches.)
- Long life lithium back-up memory battery
- True wall mount or desk use capability
- Lighting for use in the dark
- Two tone ringer for pleasant sound
- Tone Feedback on pushbutton pulse models so you know each key was fully pressed

MANUFACTURER BACKING. It's a must. Choose a brand that you know and trust. Look at the warranties. Are they limited or full? How do you get the phone serviced? What does it cost? How long will it take?

4

5

Representative inside spread

Extension Phones

2-9100 Full Feature Extension Phone
Choose the 2-9100 for Versa-dial Pulse dialing (See page 8).

2-9110 Full Feature Extension Phone
Add the convenience of a new extension.
Choose the 2-9110 for Pulse/Tone switchable dialing. (See page 8).

(TWO-YEAR WARRANTY)

MainFone™ Series

2-9250 and 2-9260 "Hotline" 12 Number Memory Phones
Choose the 2-9250 for Versa-dial Pulse dialing or 2-9260 for switchable true Tone or Pulse dialing.
3 separate One-touch emergency numbers.

2-9350 Performance Speakerphone with 12 Number Memory
Replace your telephone —
Add Hands Free and group conversation convenience.
Handset for private conversations, too!

2-9280 16 Number Instant Access Memory Dialer with Auto Busy Redial
Replace your telephone —
Add automatic dialing and end the "busy # blues".
Separate callback ringer alerts you when line is open.
Calls back busy numbers automatically.

(TWO-YEAR WARRANTY)

13

Courtesy of General Electric Company

Representative inside spread

When there's a difficult choice to be made at the sales counter between similar products, who wouldn't appreciate some help? In understaffed mass merchandising stores, where most telephones are sold, help has to come in the form of literature. So whichever company provides the most convincing and helpful literature stands the best chance of getting the sale.

That's why GE has provided this well-done guide to the many decisions facing the shopper. Why buy at all? How to select? What are the installation options? What models are available? In effect, GE has provided its own representative, in the form of inexpensive literature, to help the customer out.

This literature contains the type of detailed knowledge knows only to an industry leader. Conveying this message of leadership is the literature's primary objective. Secondarily, it serves as a vehicle for presenting all the choices in the GE line.

Organization: Priscilla.
Product: Wedding Gowns.
Literature type: 16-page sales brochure.
Use: Answer ad inquiries.

Cover

Courtesy of Priscilla

Inside spread

Although literature usually is used to provide the rationale and specific detail a potential buyer wants before making a decision, it can also be used to set or enhance the mood for an emotional sale.

For example, Priscilla doesn't sell wedding gowns, it sells romance. It's hard to read this brochure without feeling so inclined.

Ads in bridal magazines attract prospects' interest, but Priscilla realizes that it is necessary to sustain this interest and get the prospect into a bridal salon to be sold—sometimes months or years later. That's the function of this literature. It takes the initial interest created by the ad and builds upon it to create the special mood needed to get the bride-to-be to consider a Priscilla gown. Note the romantic style, soft-focus photos, and elegant design.

Organization: The Faxon Company.
Product: Library Subscription Services.
Literature type: 6-page small brochure with reply card/16-page capability brochure.
Use: Qualify prospects and provide information.

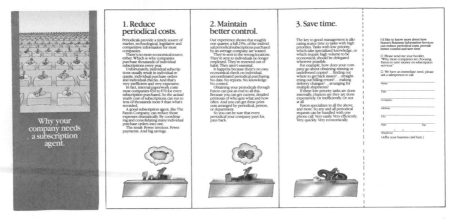

Small brochure cover   Inside spread

Sometimes selling a product or service requires an expensive two-phase sell. First a prospect has to be convinced of the need for the type of product or service. Then, he or she has to be sold on why to purchase that product or service from *your* company.

That's the challenge The Faxon Company addresses economically with two companion pieces of literature. Faxon's business is selling magazine subscription services, in this case to corporations.

The small brochure presents the rationale for "why a subscription service" in a direct and persuasive way, and by so doing qualifies a prospect. It also briefly introduces Faxon and provides a reply card which can be used to request the larger capability brochure. Using two similar but different literature pieces in this qualification/information/selling process reduces costs and considerably enhances the chance of sales success.

Capability brochure cover

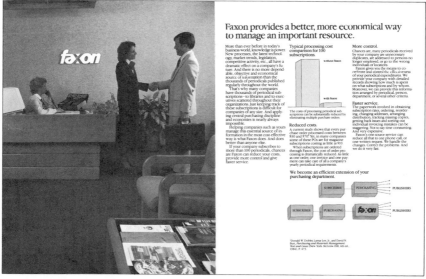

Courtesy of The Faxon Company

Representative inside spread

Organization:	Raytheon Company.
Product:	Various.
Literature type:	Quarterly house magazine.
Use:	Mailed to employees, customers, shareholders, and interested public.

Cover

Courtesy of Raytheon Company

Representative inside spread

Although expensive to produce, house magazines can be a very inexpensive way to provide a large audience with a complimentary view of a company and its products. This one well illustrates how it's done.

Raytheon is a diversified manufacturing company heavily oriented around defense electronics. Many of its employees, customers, shareholders, and neighbors know of only a small part of the company's business. Also, as one of the largest suppliers to the United States military, it needs to constantly demonstrate its capabilities, sophistication, and sound business footing to the government.

The writing and design of *Raytheon Magazine* puts a friendly, informal face on this otherwise forbidding organization. For shareholders, securities analysts, and others it makes the company look even more diversified than it really is. It builds internal *esprit de corps.* And it helps to continually reassure U.S. Department of Defense auditors that the government's money is in safe hands.

Organization: U.S. Internal Revenue Service.
Product: Income Tax.
Literature type: 48-page brochure.
Use: Taxpayer information.

Cover

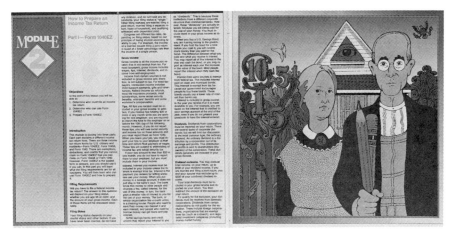

Representative inside spread

Here's a brochure that proves the power literature can have in minimizing costly customer unhappiness. Anyone reading this piece will find it belies many of his feelings about big, impersonal organizations. It is produced by the most loathsome of government departments simply to be helpful!

This brochure should provide inspiration to all organizations who deal in a product or service with potentially negative customer perceptions—or any organization which wants to keep that from becoming the case. Producing literature to reduce complaints and unhappiness resulting from misunderstandings can be a very inexpensive way to avoid costly long-term problems.

Organization: Henri's Food Products Company.
Product: Salad Dressing.
Literature type: Point-of-purchase folder.
Use: Food store rack dispensing.

Cover

Courtesy of Henri's Food Products Company

Inside spread

This illustrates the one occasion in which literature can be used to *announce* a product more cost-effectively than other promotional media. The announcement takes place right at the point-of-purchase, and the product can be easily purchased on impulse. If done well, the result is at the very least, low-cost awareness; at most it is significant new sales.

This piece quickly increases both awareness and impulse sales. The black-and-white cover is intriguing. The use of color inside creates immediate brand identity. The copy is short, as it should be, but also mouth-wateringly persuasive.

Organization: Mitsubishi.
Product: Televisions.
Literature type: 20-page sales brochure.
Use: Answer ad inquiries.

Brochure cover

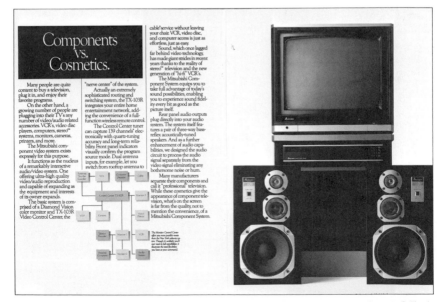

Representative inside spread

Magazine spread

In the magazine ad above, Mitsubishi seeks to position itself as the intellectual's TV. A filmmaking celebrity simply tells what he believes TV should be, and Mitsubishi promises the reader that it "accepts the challenge."

The selling comes later via the brochure that is prominently offered. And in it, the selling is hard. The brochure provides all the rationale for purchasing a Mitsubishi television. It also shows the available models.

This combination of a carefully crafted ad to attract the interest of the intellectual reader, and a brochure to provide that reader with extensive detail and rationale, can be very effective. It allows a much more targeted and hard-hitting sales presentation. It is initially more expensive than an ad alone (ad plus brochure plus mailing costs), but because it selects its audience carefully and addresses their interests specifically, the total promotional *cost per unit sold* is probably lower. This is an excellent example of the use of literature as advertising collateral.

Organization: Boston Beer Company.
Product: Samuel Adams Beer.
Literature type: Point-of-purchase tag.
Use: Attached to product.

Front cover

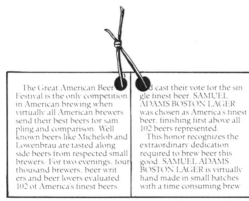

The Great American Beer Festival is the only competition in American brewing when virtually all American brewers send their best beers for sampling and comparison. Well known beers like Michelob and Lowenbrau are tasted along side beers from respected small brewers. For two evenings, four thousand brewers, beer writers and beer lovers evaluated 102 of America's finest beers

d cast their vote for the single finest beer. SAMUEL ADAMS BOSTON LAGER was chosen as America's finest beer, finishing first above all 102 beers represented.
This honor recognizes the extraordinary dedication required to brew beer this good. SAMUEL ADAMS BOSTON LAGER is virtually hand made in small batches with a time consuming brew

Courtesy of Boston Beer Company

Inside spread

ing process no longer used by American breweries. This pure beer is brewed from only the four classic ingredients: pure water, two row barley malt, Bavarian hops and lager yeast.
I hope you will appreciate the taste and character which earned SAMUEL ADAMS its selection as the Best Beer in America.
James Koch
Boston Beer Company

Back cover

What would you do if you had a small, local brewery with a limited advertising budget whose only product had just been voted the best beer in America? How could you best capitalize on the event quickly, at minimum expense, and with maximum impact?

The answer: Simply print some tags announcing the event and hang them on every bottle of beer that leaves the brewery. The only cost would be a few thousand dollars in printing and labor—no media selection, and no lengthy production time. As the only tagged product in the display case, there is assured impact on the right audience. The tag provides as much room to tell a story convincingly as any print advertisement or TV commercial

This innovative use of literature provides the Boston Beer Company with most of the selling benefits of more traditional promotional media at a fraction of the cost.

Organization:	EnMasse Computer Corporation.
Product:	Computers.
Literature type:	10-page sales brochure.
Use:	Response to inquiries.

Cover

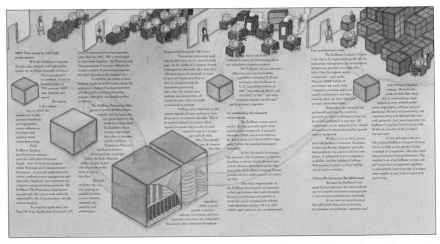

Courtesy of EnMasse Computer Corporation

Representative inside spread

Who decreed that all literature for high-tech products should look "techy," be written in engineering lingo, and be crowded with specifications? There are many steps leading up to the sale of most large-ticket, complex products. So perhaps the best way to start—to attract initial interest and move the customer to request specifications and a demonstration—is to first explain in an interesting way what is offered that is different. In other words, not to get bogged down in details prematurely.

That's what this brochure avoids. It introduces a new concept called integrated transaction management by explaining an industry problem, then offering the solution. Perhaps more importantly, it does so in a way that is visually warm and friendly. The immediate impression is of integration, expandability, and ease of use—everything EnMasse wants you to remember. And within the copy is just enough technical talk of gigabytes and Mbits to make this impression very believable.

Organization: Borden Chemical.
Product: Wallcoverings.
Literature type: 12-page decorating guide/8-page installation guide.
Use: Point-of-purchase display.

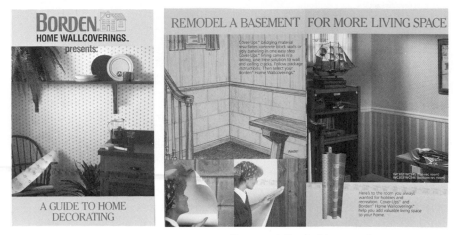

Decorating guide cover   Representative inside spread

Borden has chosen to sell a line of home wallcoverings in discount stores from a free-standing display rack. But discount stores are very concerned about return-per-square-foot of display space, so success in this endeavor depends upon sales volume, and in turn that depends upon convincing the potential buyer that it is possible to do a good job at both selecting and hanging.

In discount stores there are no experienced clerks, as there are in

Installation guide cover   Representative inside spread

paint and home furnishing stores. Thus, much of the success of this new marketing channel for Borden depends upon literature that can interest, inform, and instruct. Especially since nothing will kill this opportunity faster than too many customer returns.

These two literature pieces, prominently displayed side by side below the rolls of wallcovering, do their jobs very well. Each is visually distinct from the other and is inviting and easy to read.

Organization: Digital Marine Electronics.
Product: Northstar Loran.
Literature type: 56-page instruction manual.
Use: Backup to sales demonstrations; answer inquiries.

Cover

Inside spread

PREFACE

Your Northstar 800 Loran-C Receiver is carefully designed to provide many hours of dependable and safe navigation. But you must learn to operate your Northstar 800 with proficiency and confidence to fully enjoy its benefits. This manual introduces the Northstar 800 and helps you gain the knowledge and proficiency to operate your Northstar 800 and receive maximum benefit from the Loran-C system.

If this is your first experience with Loran-C navigation, read *SECTION 1, INTRODUCTION TO LORAN-C*, which summarizes the USCG Loran-C User Handbook. It is very important that you understand the basic principles of Loran-C navigation before you attempt to operate your Northstar 800. The sections which follow SECTION 1 assume you are familiar with the basic principles of Loran-C navigation.

SECTIONS 2 through 9 introduce basic functions of your Northstar 800 Loran-C Receiver. You should read these sections very carefully to learn how to use the front panel controls to perform some of the basic functions of your Northstar 800. Practice each function until you understand the function and corresponding readout displays. After learning the functions of the controls and readouts on the front panel, you will quickly develop the skill and relaxed confidence necessary to safely navigate your vessel with the Northstar 800.

SECTIONS 10 through 16 present advanced navigation concepts and functions of the Northstar 800.

CAUTION

A single navigational device should never be completely relied upon by the master or navigator of a vessel, to the extent that the safety of the vessel, passengers, and/or crew is put in jeopardy.

Navigational aids are just that, aids, and must be utilized as such. Information from navigational aids should be analyzed and cross checked against each other to determine the reliability of this information in plotting one's position.

The Loran-C to Loran-A conversion performed by the Northstar 800 is intended only as a convenience for the user. The Loran-A coordinates are calculated by a mathematical conversion from the Loran-C TD's. Substantial errors may exist in many cases, and the user should verify the accuracy of the converted Loran-A coordinates in his area before using them.

The steering directions obtained from the route-following features of the Northstar are intended only as a convenience to the user and should not be relied upon as the only means of navigation. In addition, the waypoint storage of the Northstar 800 should not be used as the only method of recording any important positions which the user must return to (such as the locations of lobster traps), since a failure of the unit might result in the loss of this data.

Digital Marine Electronics Corporation assumes no responsibility for losses caused by failing to observe the above precautions.

LIMITED WARRANTY

Digital Marine Electronics Corporation warrants its products to be free from defects in material and workmanship for a period of three (3) years from the date of sale by our authorized dealer to an original purchaser or subsequent owner.

This warranty covers repair and/or replacement, at our option, of any part or parts found to be defective, provided such defects in our opinion are due to faulty material or workmanship and not caused by tampering, abuse, or normal wear.

All warranties are F.O.B. Digital Marine Electronics Corporation, Acton, Massachusetts. No charges outside of DMEC will be accepted.

This warranty applies only to products in normal use. It does not apply to units or circuit boards defective due to improper installation, physical damage or tampering, receivers or mainframes subjected to fresh water or salt water immersion or spray*, units with altered serial numbers, units repaired by unauthorized persons or in violation of DMEC service procedures.

The foregoing are the only warranties expressed or implied. No other warranties exist.

Digital Marine Electronics Corporation assumes no responsibility for any consequential losses or damages of any nature with respect to any product or service sold, rendered or delivered.

NOTICE

READ THIS BEFORE YOU BUY A LORAN-C NAVIGATOR

This complimentary Owner's Manual is intended to show the reader the many navigational features and functions of the Northstar 800, and to illustrate the ease of using a Northstar 800. Indeed, the Northstar 800 is the easiest to use of all Loran-C navigators, and after reading this manual you will be capable of using a Northstar 800 with confidence.

This manual is not the one you receive when you buy a Northstar 800. The sections concerning SERVICE, TROUBLESHOOTING, INSTALLATION and INTERFACING with other Electronic Equipment has been deleted. When you purchase a Northstar 800 you receive the full manual, spiral bound with a tough plastic cover.

AFTER YOU READ THIS MANUAL TRY A NORTH-STAR 800 and COMPARE IT WITH OTHER UNITS

Go to your local Northstar dealer, test the 800 and compare it with other units. Also compare this manual with our competitors. You will quickly see which one is easier to understand, and more importantly which Loran-C navigator is the easiest to use.

AFTER YOU COMPARE YOU WILL FIND THAT THE NORTHSTAR 800 HAS:

- **BEST LAT/LONG ACCURACY** with most precise ASF corrections.

- **MOST POWERFUL RECEIVER** gives position where others can't: in fringe areas, fog, rain and dead of night.

- **BEST ROUTE and WAYPOINT SYSTEM** easiest to use, no one else comes close.

- **FASTEST RESPONSE** many receivers take several minutes to update navigation data.

- **BEST PERFORMANCE AND RELIABILITY** Northstars have won the National Marine Electronics Association's Loran-C award for 7 years in a row. And the Coast Guard (which operates the Loran-C transmitting system) uses Northstar designed and built Loran-C navigators on all of their vessels.

- **BEST WARRANTY** Three full years limited warranty on all parts and labor.

FOLLOW THE

NORTHSTAR

IT'S EASY

Instruction manuals for highly technical products are a necessity. Companies with a well-developed marketing strategy know that when manuals are understandable and helpful they produce happy customers, and happy customers produce repeat business and word-of-mouth advertising, the least expensive kind.

But good manuals are expensive, and because many preparation and production costs are fixed, it makes sense to amortize as much of this expense over as many uses as possible. That's what Digital Marine has done here with good results.

This is a cheaply printed version of most of the manual that Digital Marine packs with the product. It is distributed to potential customers *before the sale* to show just how easy to use this complex equipment is. After all, what could provide a more credible demonstration of the manufacturer's faith in his product than willingness to share the actual usage instructions that come packed with it?

Part Two

Tactics for Producing
Good Literature

CHAPTER 8

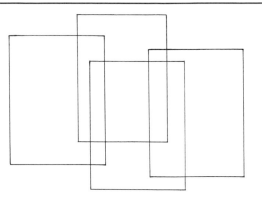

Developing the Concept

One of the keys to success in most endeavors is the degree to which strategy and tactics are differentiated. Of course, setting strategy is deciding what to do, planning tactics is deciding how to do it.

Part One covered many of the considerations necessary to the adoption of a literature strategy. In Part Two we now take up literature tactics, which involve creativity. Although creativity is obviously a gift that cannot be bestowed, craftlike aspects of creativity can be learned. In addition, the creative process can be stimulated. It is possible to learn from past experience and to develop guidelines to raise the creative batting average.

This first chapter in Part Two covers the vital first step in the creative process. It is the development of a *concept*—the expression, usually visual but sometimes written, of what the actual literature will be like. The concept is both a statement of the strategy and a blueprint for the tactics that will make it happen. Further definition of a concept is provided in the Glossary.

The concept can be thought of as the necessary transition between communication strategy and creative tactics. Another way of putting it is that the concept is the creative *positioning* of the literature.

Regardless of how it is expressed, the concept is by far the most important aspect of the creative process. No amount of effort based on poor strategy is ever truly effective; and no amount of good writing, design, photography, or printing can rescue literature constructed around a poor concept.

DEFINE OBJECTIVES

Can a strong literature concept be developed without first developing equally strong objectives? Probably not, even though not too many creative people will admit it.

In fact, to even mention objectives frightens most writers and designers. With considerable justification, they feel that too much emphasis on cold, objective data leads inevitably to materials which meet every criteria except one: success. Or that the success is minor compared to what could have been achieved in a more freethinking environment.

Do strong, precise objectives necessarily have to produce the same effect on creativity that DDT has on small things that crawl and fly? And is it possible for one individual to be simultaneously creative and analytical? Can exercise of the left (analytical) side of the brain be achieved without draining the energy available to the right (creative) side? No—and yes; it all depends on the rigidity with which the objectives are defined.

With too much rigidity and too many rules, creativity will surely suffer. We must never forget that the most powerful ideas in any creative medium always come from breaking the rules; from an intuitive feel about what is right and what works best.

But we must also be aware that few of the people engaged in any creative endeavor are gifted enough to possess that intuition. This is particularly true in the literature medium, which has not always attracted the top creative talent.

Without objectives, we are dealing with nothing more than raw luck. And luck has no place in any activity bought and paid for with a purpose in mind. To paraphrase whichever general it was, "Luck has no more place in literature than in warfare."

Enough, then, about justifying the need for objectives. Defining objectives is the necessary first step in developing a concept. And because the objectives for any given literature piece must be subordinate to the objectives of a larger communications or marketing plan, we must proceed here on the assumption that such a master plan exists.

The objectives for a single literature piece should be neither rigid in construction, nor long in words. All they need to do is provide simple answers to the following:

- What is the purpose of the piece?
- Who is the typical reader?
- Why will the reader benefit from reading the piece?
- What type of action is desired of the reader?
- How does this action support other objectives (such as sales quotas)?
- How will the literature mesh with other communications media?
- What other factors need to be considered (product positioning, company image, and so forth)?

A single sentence addressing each of these points is all that's necessary. In fact, it can be argued that actually writing down an objective statement is not necessary; that the discipline of defining the objective, not recording it, is what is important. As true as this is, a written objective does provide a basis for others to work with, a record for the preparer to rely upon later, and an assurance that the written objectives of other communications media are in synch.

A written paragraph that incorporates each of the points above will probably prevent one of the biggest problems in literature—that of inappropriate creativity looking around for a home.

Too often, a particular idea, a pet brainchild of a member of the creative team, will be applied to the next project that happens to come along. Sometimes, too, the creative approach developed for another medium is simply adapted to the literature. In either case, the result, while creative, doesn't work because it doesn't communicate the proper message.

To assure that this doesn't happen, under no circumstances should a concept or creative idea be entertained until the literature's need has been defined, and its objectives have been determined. Only then will there be an accurate way to determine what will work, and why.

CONSIDER LIMITATIONS

Once the objectives have been determined, the next step in developing the concept is to consider the limitations and parameters to which the literature must conform.

The following should always be included. And in addition to these points, each organization, each specific literature need, will generate its own list of items which should be considered before the concept is actually developed.

Budget. This is perhaps the most important consideration: What is affordable? The ideal concept is the one which meets the need in the most cost-effective way. But, unfortunately, in most situations the ideal is not possible. Rather, it is necessary to work within a budgeted amount. Size, length, paper, illustrations, color, printing, and distribution are all affected.

Information. It does little good to conceive of a 16-page selling brochure if there is only enough information available for a two-sided product sheet. Or to conceive of a two-sided product sheet if there is information, need, and budget for a 16-page selling brochure.

Time. How much is available? Does the literature have to be produced for a particular occasion? If so, does that limit the availability of certain information, or illustrations? Does it also force the use of certain creative people, or the use of certain production equipment?

Need. Can the story best be told visually, with many illustrations and few words? Or can it best be told with many words and few illustrations? Should the designer be the lead member of the creative team, or the writer? Who initiates the conceptual thinking?

Use. Will the literature be used or distributed in a particular way? Does it have to fit in a binder, or a particular-sized envelope? Will it be passed along to multiple readers, or will it be read once and thrown away?

Organizational Style. Are there standards for writing and design which must be considered? Do certain trademarks or trade names need to be treated in a specific way? Are you bound into the use of certain grids, formats, or colors?

Quantity. A concept for a literature piece originally planned for production in large quantities, with significant economies of scale, may be an economic disaster if produced in small quantities; and vice versa.

After these and other items have been considered, the next step will be to actually start the creative process. But before doing that, it is also worth quickly considering the ability of the human mind to retain and recall information.

Psychologists tell us that without frequent review we forget more than 80 percent of all we learn within 24 hours, and we forget nearly everything within a few days. Moreover, our brains store information in mind patterns, chunks of information organized around key words and images. And the faster we can read something, in both a literal and visual sense, the easier it is for these patterns to form, and the more we will be able to recall later.

For these reasons and more, *it is critically important that the concept focus around a single key idea, and that this idea be broken into a few easily digestible components.*

FOCUS ON ONE IDEA

The best way to assure that you start immediately to focus upon the single best idea for the concept is to ask the question: What is the *one* point I want to stay with the reader—forever.

Perhaps it is something general: economy, or value, or innovation, or leadership. Perhaps it is something specific: a major product benefit, a new capability, improved service. Make sure that you can verbalize the thought in a single, simple, and direct statement. Remember, use only one thought—in a simple declarative sentence. For example: "Acme faucets are guaranteed dripless."

Then look for the most intriguing, memorable way to make

that single point in words and visuals. Perhaps a photograph showing a guarantee under a faucet with this headline, "Turn off the water. If our guarantee gets wet, we'll send you a new faucet—anytime." Now, build the concept around this theme. Relate everything—facts, detail, photography, and graphics—to reliability.

CREATE THE UNUSUAL

Keep in mind that unlike advertising, sales promotion, or direct mail, the concept does not have to arrest attention or entertain. But it should be both memorable and believable. The more creative the concept is, the more potential it has to make the literature dollar work harder; nothing more, nothing less.

Unfortunately, a great deal of this creativity—which we'll define here as the establishing of differentness, thence memorability—fails. One major reason is that too often creativity becomes an end in itself, rather than a tool of good communications. Although most creative people will eschew this, the problem persists because of the difficulty in keeping perspective. A great idea often comes to have a life of its own, even though it may be totally inappropriate to the need.

Sometimes the fault lies in not getting a clear enough picture of what the literature has to accomplish. This can be caused by a lack of clear objectives or a lack of business experience on the part of the person undertaking the assignment. It can also be due to simple ignorance or arrogance on the part of the creative team.

On some occasions, creative failure comes from ignorance of the specific problems and opportunities unique to the literature medium. This tends to be especially true in organizations where literature is considered to have low prestige and is assigned to the most junior personnel. Too many literature concepts suffer from either misdirected creativity, or creative ennui, or both.

The sharper, the more focused the message, the easier it will be to see whether it is on target or not. More important, the sharper the message, the more likely it will stay in the readers' consciousness. In deciding what this message, the creative concept, should be, consider that ideas which *reinforce* readers' perceptions have a far better chance of being believed and recalled than those which challenge it. In general, the mind tends to accept most readily that which, in some way, corresponds to prior knowledge and experience.

Direct challenges to preconceived notions often work very well in attracting attention, but usually do a very poor job of persuading. So, except in rare cases, don't be contentious. Don't try to change an opinion, or reposition a product through confrontation, no matter how valid. At this time you should play to the readers' perceptions and interests.

Later, in the development of the copy and design, there will be ample opportunities to subtly change opinions. But unless the concept actively encourages readership, the reader will never get to that point.

MAKE IT INTERESTING

If possible, orient the concept around whatever is different about the product or service. Around what adman Rosser Reeves called the *USP—the Unique Selling Proposition*. Then, make the USP interesting.

Offer an implicit reward for reading—a challenge, a promise of needed information. You are asking the reader to spend time with you. Show why it's in the reader's interest. There are several techniques which can be employed to help make the concept interesting.

"Breakthrough" Creativity.   The right creative approach is essential to making literature attractive, readable, and memorable. Breakthrough creativity goes beyond even this. It results in a literature piece so different, that it stands apart and isn't easily forgotten. Through strikingly unusual graphics, photography, or words, it does more than simply provide the best stage for communication. It *becomes* the communication.

The advantages of such attention getting and impact are obvious. But there are potential disadvantages in the attempt to be unique as well. Do you really have the talent to pull it off? Will the reader remember the artistry but forget the message? Will the extra cost justify the increased visibility?

Demonstration.   How easily can the product be demonstrated in a few photographs? How easily can its unique operation be explained in a few words? How interesting will either be to the reader?

If it is possible to answer, "very" to each of these three questions, perhaps the concept should focus around a product demonstration. Or at least it should include a product demonstration. In either case, it is important not to try to demonstrate too many features; one or two are all that can be handled well. And always make sure you are demonstrating something important to the reader, not something important to you, the seller.

Testimonials.   The words of others, especially experts in a field, usually carry far more weight than our own. They provide a strong dose of credibility and are particularly appropriate whenever you want to make a single claim very believable.

In addition, testimonials provide a way of quickly focusing interest on certain features. They are especially good as a tie-in to other media, such as ads (by using the same spokespeople, for example). Using quotes and writing in the first person also lends style and interest to what might otherwise be dull prose.

There are two caveats: (1) To be successful, testimonials cannot be used repeatedly in an organization's literature; so, save them for the concepts that really need them. (2) Make sure you discuss the idea with legal counsel; there are very specific rules on the use of testimonials, especially when celebrities are involved.

Case History.   A case history is an extended testimonial showing how an organization or group uses specific products or services. A concept can be organized around a single case history, or more likely, around several mini-case histories which show products being used in a variety of actual situations.

The value of a case history is directly related to the prestige of the featured user. At its best, a case history is a very effective way to present a story. However, it is often difficult to arrange, and even harder to actually execute. The right organization(s) must be found and agree to be profiled; and the organization must be happy later with the resulting publicity.

Not as effective, but worth considering because it is more practical and allows more creative freedom, is the use of *hypo-*

thetical case histories—typical examples of the way in which the product is actually used.

Sex.   Contrary to what many marketers of items as varied as machine tools and lawn equipment apparently believe, sex is not very effective in helping to communicate the features and benefits of most products. Usually it simply diverts attention from the literature's message. The reader remembers the woman or man but not the product or its features.

It should also be recognized, however, that sex can be a very powerful technique when the literature deals with a product designed to create sexual allure (such as perfume or lingerie), or with a product that has strong sexual undertones (such as an automobile).

As a general rule, a concept which features gratuitous sex will create interest and titillate but will do a very poor job of communicating. On the other hand, a concept that builds on the unique capacity of the product to create sexual allure or satisfy subliminal sexual fantasies will probably be very successful.

People.   People are involved in all products. Moreover, they are the key to success for many organizations, especially service businesses. For this reason a concept which spotlights an organization's staff can be very effective.

To work, the concept has to focus on what makes the staff different from others in similar businesses. For example, their unique experience, education, or responsibility; or the way the firm's staff is organized; or their friendliness.

Most important, the concept must build upon the truth. There is nothing more disastrous than literature which extols an organization's prompt and friendly service when the world knows the service is actually tardy and surly.

Transferred Meanings.   Some words, phrases, and images are naturally associated in our mind with particular items, events, or timing. When they are used outside their normal context, interest focuses immediately.

For example, "the wettest spot in the desert," a concept for literature showing humidifiers photographed in a desert home, would work well. The statement attracts attention because it belies the popular notion of dry, desertlike conditions.

Concepts which redefine accepted notions, or which take advantage of double meanings, stake out a unique preemptive position for the product and create strong memorability.

Each of these techniques is but one way to make the message of a literature piece appealing and interesting. There are countless additional ways, as well. And for much literature nothing more than a straightforward product description is necessary.

TEST FOR EFFECTIVENESS

Once the concept has been decided, it should be tested. Regardless of its focus or complexity, every concept should be able to pass at least this test: *Can the name of a similar product or service be easily substituted?* If it can, the concept probably isn't as strong as it should be; scrap it. Go back and try again.

Only when you cannot substitute another name—because the conceptual statement being made is unique to the product or service—has the concept passed this very important first test for effectiveness. At that point, it should also be tested against these other criteria:

- Does it fit all objectives and plans?
- Does it take into account the weaknesses as well as the strengths of the product or service?
- Does it address reader interests, as opposed to your interests?
- Can it be done within the time and budget allocated?
- Does it have interest and story appeal?
- Does it build upon the organization's image or personality?
- Does it have staying power, or will it be quickly outdated?

REFINE THE APPROACH

It is said that when one is looking for something really good, one has to travel slowly. When you are satisfied that the concept is effective, and that it can meet the objectives, fit the budget, accommodate the information, be produced on time, and be appropriate to the use required—it's time to forget it for awhile.

Put the concept aside for a day or two, a week if you have the luxury of time. Don't look at. Don't think about it. Then bring it out and, once again, evaluate it as objectively as possible. Do you still like it? Is it the best single approach to the requirements and constraints under which you must work? If not, refine it until it works. But don't start over. Keep the same approach, preserve the essence, just make it work better. The reason not to start over is that you will probably toss out a good, strong idea for something more conservative, something safer.

Timid concepts do a poor job of communicating. So to second-guess your own creativity at this time will most likely be self-defeating. Go with your original gut feeling for what is right. Simply refine the presentation; perhaps change the page order, replace the headlines, fiddle with the graphics—not much else. Don't study or refine it to death.

Then, and only then, show the concept to a few select peers, preferably other professionals who can judge it on its communications ability, without knowledge of the constraints under which it was developed. Do they like it? Do they have any appropriate, minor suggestions for improvement, or do all the suggestions require conditions such as a larger budget that are either improbable or impossible? If done informally and limited to a few knowledgeable persons, such a creative review can be very helpful by pointing out obvious problems that often go unnoticed by someone close to the project.

In any event, the concept must be zealously protected against *consensus creativity.* No concept will please all individuals equally, so no attempt should be made to accommodate all points of view. A creative review will only help in the development of good concepts when it is viewed as a refinement step, not as a process for making major changes.

OBTAIN APPROVAL

Approval procedures differ widely from one organization to another. Even within a single organization, procedures vary according to the complexity and potential impact of the literature.

It is hard to imagine top officers of a corporation not wishing to approve the concept for an annual report before any extensive writing, photography, or design work is done. It is also difficult to visualize any large organization where the approval of several executives is required on the concept for a simple bill stuffer.

In general, any significant literature project should have concept approval before its writing and design is undertaken. Ideally, this approval will be informal and limited to a few key individuals who will judge the concept for its marketing direction and communications impact. This initial approval will assure that the project is headed in the right direction before it has proceeded too far. Later routing of copy and design will accommodate the need to check style and the accuracy of facts and details. Very specific guidelines on approval review procedures are provided in Appendix One.

CHAPTER 9

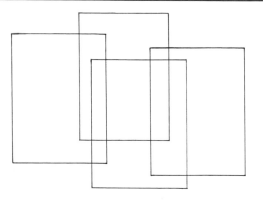

Words That Persuade: Outlining, Writing, and Rewriting

After concept approval it's time to completely cross the bridge from strategy to tactics; time to consider the details of literature preparation—the writing, design, production, and distribution.

If the approved concept is a highly visual one, one which requires mainly photographs or illustrations, design considerations should come next. But for most literature, words provide the organization and structure, and writing should be considered first. Thus, this chapter on writing precedes the one on design.

It is worth emphasizing that the processes of conceptualizing, writing, and designing are seldom undertaken as separate functions. It is best and often critical for writer and designer to interact at all stages of the literature's development. The process should never be as linear or as independent as it is presented here.

Perhaps the first step in any discussion about the development of the words (copy) in literature is to dispel any negative notion about their value. A belief often voiced today by an unsophisticated but vocal minority is that we live in a visual world where words don't really matter much any more. This belief becomes manifest in such statements as, "Don't worry now about the copy, just leave enough room and we'll fill it in later. Most people don't read it anyway."

If you accept such simplistic reasoning, it is doubtful that your literature will ever be effective. Literature, more than any other medium with the possible exception of direct mail, caters to the interest of the reader. The only time copy isn't read is when it is dull and boring.

Copy is always important in literature. We may, indeed, live in an increasingly visual world, but we also live in an increasingly literate one in which more books and more magazines are sold every year. More promotional literature, with more copy, is produced every year, too.

An attempt *will* be made to read the copy in your literature. The copy will influence the reader one way or another, and it will or it will not provide the basis for decision making. Anything less than the most powerful and provocative words you can use is a mistake.

KNOW WHAT IS EXPECTED

Regardless of what other functions you may actually perform in your organization, for the balance of this chapter, you are now a copywriter. If you normally do write copy, what follows will be lots of review and reaffirmation and perhaps a few new ideas. If you normally review copy written by others, becoming briefly immersed in the writing process should help immeasurably in allowing you to do better reviewing.

As a copywriter, you're in very good company. In the marketing communications business, this is the original art, much polished and perfected over the years. Moreover, within the literature medium you are in an environment where the power of a phrase and the cadence of text remain paramount.

Precisely because literature is a writer's medium, and because there is a long history of what works, the writer carries a lot of responsibility for success. Therefore it is important to remind ourselves from time to time exactly what is expected of us.

The job of copywriter is not to write copy, any more than the job of a bus driver is to drive a bus. The job of a bus driver is to transport people, and the job of a copywriter is to interest, inform, or persuade readers. At the very least, a copywriter's efforts should impart knowledge; at most, they should result in a specific action. Nor is the objective of the copywriter great writing. The objective is some designated knowledge or action, and writing is merely the means by which it is partially attained. Sometimes great writing helps this process, sometimes it merely gets in the way of the message.

In most cases, literature copywriting is simply the art of persuasion practiced through the printed word. There are exceptions, such as when the only objective is the imparting of knowledge, but usually copywriting is simply "salesmanship in print."—Nothing but. Every copywriter should repeat that a dozen times every single morning.

TAKE ALL THE HELP YOU CAN GET

Good copywriting is difficult with help; it is next to impossible without help. Don't make things any harder than they have to be. The easier the words come, the better they will be, and the more you will live to produce.

Compile a Library of Sources.   Creativity can come from many sources, and one of the least effective for most of us is our own mind. "Nothing is original in the world" may be a cliche, but that doesn't make it any less true. After millennia of thinking, centuries of writing, and decades of promotional literature, anyone not using the previous work of others as a source of inspiration is simply not doing things the right way, regardless of how creative he believes he is.

Inspiration and organization always come faster and better to those who look at what others have done in a similar situation, gather bits and pieces from here and there, mold these to their own ends, and from them create something unique.

This process is usually faster and more efficient than trying to come up with everything from your own mind. Remember, copywriting is the business of writing for money, so the faster something good can be produced, the better. No one, writer or client, benefits in a situation where it takes many times longer to come up with an idea that's just a little more original.

Avoid the Temptations to Plagiarize.   The preceding advice should not be construed as an endorsement of outright plagiarism—the use of the exact phrases of another in a similar context.

This warning about plagiarism has nothing to do with the law. As time goes on, more and more is written and printed and it becomes harder and harder to prove intent to plagiarize. This is especially true in the arena of mass communications where fad and fashion are so important. The legal risk of plagiarizing is really very small.

The concern is not primarily ethical, either. Rather, it is based on the simple, pragmatic fact that plagiarism usually backfires. First, the better the stolen words are, the more likely they are to be unique to the needs of the originator; chances are they won't work as well for you. Second, and perhaps more importantly, stealing words is a creative cop-out which indicates an ennui which inevitably shows up in far more than just inappropriate copy.

Tap All Available Technology.   We all have our writing idiosyncrasies, and some seem truly important to our creativity. But they usually function as crutches and limitations, especially when it is necessary to produce work on a time schedule.

A copywriter who is producing literature does not have the luxury of time enjoyed by a poet or novelist. Like journalists and others working under the pressure of deadlines, the assignments must get out on time, and they must be reasonably well done. Any tool, technology, or innovation that can help ideas flow and words get produced faster must be exploited. Those who think otherwise are merely rationalizing their preferences or insecurities.

The copywriter who would not use a typewriter a few generations ago had a very limited future. So, too, the copywriter of today who will not use a word processor. In the future, copywriters who resist thought-organizing software and electronic formatting and publishing systems will probably be at a similar disadvantage.

DO YOUR HOMEWORK

Any good copywriter knows that writing skill comprises only a fraction of the copywriting formula. Knowledge of the product, the reader, and the competition make up most of the formula.

It is certainly possible to write a literature piece—come up with a few acceptable headlines and fill in the body copy—with only scant knowledge. But the result is seldom effective.

We've all seen examples. The product is incorrectly positioned for its market. The piece is airy, there are few specifics, and the facts presented are wrong; the right facts are missing. The reader is soon turned off by vacuous claims and trite phrases. It's an opportunity lost, possibly forever.

Sometimes such a lost opportunity is the result of a lack of tenacity in fact gathering. Other times the problem is a lack of interviewing skill. In either case, the end product is the same: writing which may be creatively excellent but is notably devoid of strong content.

One way to minimize this problem is to spend more time on research than on the writing itself—up to several times as long. This will not only improve the content, but will make the task of writing easier and faster.

Know the Product. It is impossible to know too much about the product. It is probably impractical to compile information beyond a certain point, but that is for you to decide. Ideally, you should know enough about the product to sell it in person, but this is seldom practical.

It is, of course, possible for a copywriter to be burdened with excessive detail, but in literature the problem is usually too little, not too much. Unlike the writing of ads, the writing of literature requires lots of facts.

Too often, product information comes to the copywriter through a second- or third-hand source, which means it is passed through several filters. Even if all the facts remain, the original flavor is bound to be lost. To guard against this, the copywriter should do as much of the fact gathering as possible, and should hunt for those anecdotes and activities that can add interest and credibility to the story to be told.

This process requires a certain amount of time, a high degree of curiosity, and a willingness to get out of the office and into the boondocks. But the extra effort pays off. Digging and probing provide the source materials that allow good literature to be written—the type that is not only full of meat, but is also based on truth, hard facts, and real experiences.

Wherever possible, utilize objective test reports so you can write credibly of the product's benefits and counter the effects of its liabilities. Talk to the salespeople who have to sell it. And, most important, talk to the customers who use it.

Know the Competitions' Products.   It is not as essential to know the competitions' products as intimately as your own, but it is necessary to be familiar with them. You cannot hope to be competitive without knowing what you are up against.

What are the strengths and weaknesses of the competing products—including product specs, distribution, and service? Start with customer perceptions and objective test data, if available. Attempt to relate these to what the competitors emphasize in their literature, advertising, and promotions. Are they emphasizing strengths and downplaying weaknesses well? How do these relate to the strengths and weaknesses of your product? Does it result in a target of opportunity for your literature?

Also, examine competitors' literature and advertising for style. Make sure what you plan will look and read differently enough to give your company and product a unique identity in the marketplace. Similarities only result in customer confusion, to the detriment of all concerned.

In summary, make sure you know enough about your competitors' products to avoid their strengths and capitalize on their weaknesses.

Know the Reader.   Interesting and effective copy is written from the *reader's* point of view. Relate what you have to say to his/her interests. This is impossible if you don't know the reader and don't know the environment or market where the reader functions. People don't buy products, they buy solutions to problems. So you must first know what those problems are and how deeply they are felt. You must also know what other options the reader has been offered and how attractive they are. And you must know the price the reader is willing to pay to have the problem solved. The best way to find all this out is by field experience—intimate knowledge of customer feelings gained through talking and selling. Focus group sessions are another way, as are traditional market studies.

With any or all of these as background, try now to enter the mind of the typical reader. Then organize your material and write copy to appeal to this person, and this person alone.

In doing so, remember that in this world nearly all problems can be solved. What you really need to convince the reader of is *relative value.* That can be defined simply this way: Benefit minus price equals value $(B - P = V)$.

Know What You Should Say. From all this information you must now sift what is important from what is not important and organize a list of points which must be covered if the literature is to do a good job. This will become the foundation upon which both concept and outline will be built.

To do this, it is important that you understand all the information you have gathered well enough to state it in your own words. Doing so is particularly important, because this process integrates the information into your unique set of mental processes and firmly fixes it in your mind.

The best test for understanding is always whether you can explain a subject quickly and clearly to a friend. In this case, can you concisely explain the product's major attributes? . . . those of competitive products? . . . the fears, interests, and needs of your potential readers (customers)?

Finally, make sure that you integrate and reconcile all this new information with the information you already possess on marketing strategy and tactics.

ORGANIZE WITH AN OUTLINE

What to many copywriters is the fun part of the job—the interviewing, the fact gathering, the musing—is now over. It's time to get to work and to begin the actual process of writing.

You now face the legendary blank sheet of paper in the typewriter or, today, the blank computer screen. It has intimidated great novelists, poets, and playwrights, as well as copywriters, before you. So if you feel at a loss for where to start, you're in good company.

But as a copywriter you have a distinct advantage. You know from the homework you've done what things you must say, and you know their relative importance. All that remains is to put them in order before you actually start.

Most writers, commercial as well as artistic, do this with some sort of outline. It needn't be formal, or even written down. But the longer and the more difficult the project is, or the more unsure you are of your approach, the more important a tangible guide becomes.

If the facts you have gathered can be thought of as a foundation for the story you will build, the outline can be thought of as the framework. Together they will assure that what you construct will be solid as well as attractive.

Recognize Traditional Limitations. There are a number of outlining techniques taught in writing courses and presented in books on effective writing. There is also computer software available for organizing ideas and putting them into an outline form that can be later expanded into text.

Unfortunately, most of these outlining techniques are woefully inadequate for our purposes. This is because they organize information as if it were to be presented in book form, or in a report.

The assumption is that the reader will begin at the title page and work through to the end—word after word, page after page, chapter after chapter—in a very linear fashion.

In reading a brochure or other literature piece, however, something different actually happens. The typical reader does *not* start at the beginning and work through to the end. Instead, the reader skips around, sees headlines, and looks at illustrations; then, if he is interested, he starts to read. So the outline for literature has to be constructed accordingly.

An outline for a literature piece must assure a way of creating interest while organizing information. The outline must help make the mass of information manageable by connecting related facts, and it must make the information interesting by connecting these facts directly to reader concerns.

Organize around Benefits. For the time being, forget trying to tell an interesting story. Instead, select the single most important fact, idea, or statement about the product, make it the title of your outline.

Next, pick a half dozen key benefits—and be sure they are customer benefits, not merely product features. Make these the major sections under which you will gather all the rest of the material. Then, select the product's minor benefits; make them subsections under the major sections. Finally, sort all the information you have under these sections and subsections.

Present the Benefits in an Interesting Way. Now, keeping the same title, rearrange the sections in an interesting, logical, persuasive manner. Try to think like a successful salesperson. First, introduce the product. Then, describe what it offers and how, point to support, and provide a bridge to further action.

With the sections thus arranged, consider how much space you have to work with. Try to make one major point on each page, or even better, or each double page spread. Combine sections if necessary to make this happen. Then combine subsections so that there are only two or three in each major section.

Finally, rearrange sections to make an interesting story. One formula often followed is *AIDA:* Attention, Interest, Desire, Action. If your outline is organized to produce all four, chances are the literature will be strong and effective.

Another formula often followed is the *3-30-3* rule. It stands for 3 seconds, 30 seconds and 3 minutes—the amount of time different readers spend with literature. The 3-second reader will note only the title and perhaps one or two illustrations. The 30-second reader will note title, heads, subheads and illustrations. The 3-minute reader will note title, heads, subheads, illustrations, and copy that is of interest. Good literature is constructed around an outline that assures that each of these readers receives the strongest possible message.

DEVELOP THE CONCEPT

To emphasize its importance, the development of the concept was discussed separately in the previous chapter. Normally, however, the development of the concept or theme would follow the outlining process. Let's assume here that the concept has been approved and review only a few of its important aspects.

First, the concept should encompass a few major ideas. For it is ideas that motivate people—not writing, not design. They are merely ways to present ideas.

To be successful, a concept must register the name of the company, its product or service, a few ideas, and a few points which provide credibility. If it does this, the individuals who review the concept will be at more or less the same place as the reader of the printed literature during the first few seconds after it is picked up and perused.

The reason for this is the way readers will actually read the literature. Again, a typical reader does not start at the beginning of a piece and work through to the end reading every word. The reader scans headlines, sub-heads and illustrations while deciding subsconsciously whether to backtrack and delve in for more information. It is from this scan that lasting impressions are formed and any interest in reading the actual text is generated.

Only if the initial impression is favorable and the interest generated is high, will any of the body copy actually be read. Therefore the actual text should never be written until the head and major subhead statements—interesting, persuasive, and strategically important statements all—have been decided.

If the outline is well done, writing the heads and subheads is simply a matter of taking the sections and subsection titles and rephrasing them. In doing this, speak to the reader's interests, include product benefits wherever possible, use short sentences, and always try to incorporate a verb.

Finally, before writing the body copy repeat to yourself: *the only function of the text is to expand upon the heads and sub-heads, and to make them believable.*

SIT DOWN AND WRITE

When starting to write it is important to focus on one person, and one person only—the typical reader. Then write directly to this person and exclude all others from consideration.

Doing this is easy to the extent that you can, like a good

character actor, crawl inside the typical reader and actually assume his or her personality, interests, likes, and dislikes. Then you simply provide the information you would want, answer the questions you would raise, and do it all in a style you would respond to. Of course, this is easier said than done. But the more homework you've done, the easier it will be.

Copy Logic. Any literature piece—whether a lengthy annual report or short brochure—must tell a single, cohesive, persuasive story. But as noted previously, literature is seldom read serially, from beginning to end. So the logic of developing the copy has to be, first, to get the reader to associate all the visual elements—heads, subheads, illustrations—with an interesting and important chronology. This will encourage him or her to go back to the beginning to get the whole story.

Second, the body copy should be developed so that it not only supports the heads and subheads, but also tells a tightly woven story with a beginning, middle, and end. It must be both easy to get into and compelling enough to encourage continued readership. Like a Wagnerian opera, it must have a leitmotif or a recurring theme which, in this case, is related to customer needs.

In other words, to be successful, the literature must be developed as an organic whole, not as a collection of elements. Yet, paradoxically, it must be presented to the reader as a collection of elements (benefits) which are connected in a way which gives a complete, interesting, and credible story.

For a product, a typical story might begin by presenting introductory information, perhaps a statement of the problem facing the reader. It moves on to a description of the product and how it solves the problem. Perhaps then it discusses other applications and benefits. It continues by addressing service and backup support. It provides detailed specifications. And it ends with a bridge to further action, including a reply card, sales office addresses, and so forth.

This is not to advocate the development of copy to a formula. It is only to suggest that the copywriter recognize before starting that most readers will feel most comfortable with, and remember best, that which appears in a familiar story form with a logical beginning, middle, and end.

Copy Content.   There is usually more appropriate information available than can be used productively in any single literature piece. So deciding upon copy content is usually a process of placing relative value on the material at hand, then editing—severely.

How much information is enough, and how much is too much, is strictly a judgment call. But the tendency of most copywriters is to err on the side of more rather than less. Perhaps this is because it seems safer, or easier.

In addition, information will probably be added, not subtracted, in the approval process, further exacerbating the information overload. Frequently, individuals who review copy believe that every fact or benefit omitted will result in a potential customer loss, and they insist on adding detail.

Actually, the opposite normally happens. Too much material— a plethora of deadly facts, specifications, applications, and detail—camouflages what is really important, wearies the reader, and keeps anything from getting through. A typical literature piece is composed of many elements, and the omission of a few insights of information in the process of painting a big picture will probably never be noticed. Even if noticed, they will seldom be enough to discourage serious interest.

In most cases literature is but one step in a sales or information process and whatever deficiencies it may have can usually be made up. In any case, erring on the side of too little information in order to speed up reading and encourage interest in larger issues, is usually the lesser of two evils. All the above is best summarized by another cliche: Less really is more!

When making hard choices, always include what is novel and significant to the reader, and exclude the familiar and the obvious. Also, make sure you emphasize anything unique that can be used to establish a preemptive position in the market. If uniqueness is hard to come by, find a way to express the commonplace which makes it appear unique.

Finally, it is impossible to consider content without considering the way in which it will be presented. A reader's tolerance for detail is always directly related to how interesting it can be made. No reader wants to analyze straight facts in order to find a benefit; he expects your interpretation. Conversely, no reader want to wade through long copy in order to discover a few facts.

And that brings up the question of style.

Copy Style. In any literature there is always some dichotomy between content (substance) and style (the way the substance is presented). The more space taken up with that intangible we label style—the collective result of adjectives, transitional phrases, and anecdotes—the less space is available for product features and benefits.

With too little emphasis on writing style, the literature will be dull, boring, and ineffective. Too much emphasis on style, and the literature will be insulting to the reader and demeaning to the product. So, how do you determine what is appropriate?

In general, most literature suffers from a paucity of style. This is less true of consumer products literature than that used in the industrial or business products markets, but the latter accounts for the bulk of literature produced.

Far too little literature is written with the understanding that *how* something is said can have as much or greater impact than *what* is being said, even though our everyday experience shows this to be the case. To prove the point, consider that style in writing is directly analogous to tone of voice in speaking. Both can convey far more information than the mere words alone.

Style can strongly enhance the message, damn it with insufficient enthusiasm, or actually contradict it. It can turn the poor into mediocre, the mediocre into good, and the good into great.

Of course, producing the appropriate style for any given literature piece is directly related to copywriting talent. But craftsmanship also plays a key role, and that can be learned through experience and practice. Adhering to some time-proven principles and techniques may not produce a great copywriter, but it can help everyone do the job a lot better.

Here are some style pointers:

- Write to your typical reader in the way he or she talks. Be natural, try to avoid talking up, or talking down. Use industry or trade terms as appropriate, but avoid jargon, cliches, and pompous phrases.

- Use simple, everyday words. Involve the reader with action verbs and picture nouns. Stay away from too many adjectives; they slow down the copy. Employ emotional words such as, "you," 'new," "now," 'free." Use contractions to keep the copy loose.
- Be specific. Avoid abstractions. Words like "quality" conjure up only fuzzy images. Instead, give the reader concrete facts that prove quality. Wherever possible quantify any claims.
- Keep most sentences short, less than 15 words. But also vary sentence length. Keep one idea to a sentence. Use numbers within a compound sentence to identify a series of important points, or a series of dots (. . .) to separate thoughts.
- Keep paragraphs short and vary their length. Use one-sentence and one-word paragraphs to emphasize a point. Use bridges and connecting phrases to keep up the pace and maintain a continuous copy flow between paragraphs.
- Use bullets to call attention to points which don't fit naturally into sentence form. But remember, a list of more than 10 or so loses its effectiveness, as does more than one list per page.
- Try to have only one major headline (head) on every page or double-page spread. Never have more than about 250 words without a subhead, boldface lead, or other visual break. Pace the copy. And keep it digestible by splitting it into discrete, but connected, segments. Give the reader a chance to digest one important point before providing the next one.
- Build in reiteration. Try to make important points several different ways in several different places. Photos, captions, and anecdotal sidebars are often a good way to accomplish this.
- Be literate. Show proper respect for the English language, its structure, punctuation, and syntax. This doesn't mean you shouldn't bend the rules where appropriate, but do it out of respect for communication, not cleverness or ignorance.
- Don't be cute. Wise-guy headlines and aggressive copy

get attention, but they usually turn the reader off. Hitting the reader over the head verbally is not usually the best way to persuade. Likewise, be careful not to get carried away with your own desire to do something really creative. Avoid pet phrases and inside jokes.

- Don't be afraid of long copy as long as you can make it interesting. Don't make copy so short that it is not interesting.
- Don't be afraid of negative headlines if they reflect what's already in the reader's mind. Admit that the product is something less than perfect in the body copy. Anticipate negatives and meet the skeptical reader halfway. If the reader believes you are telling the truth, he or she will not only be willing to listen, but will do so in an atmosphere of credibility.

REVISE, REVISE, REVISE

The author once worked for one of those rare individuals who could actually dictate a first draft of copy from notes, then get everything perfect in one or two rewrites. For most of us, however, creating good copy is a much more laborious process involving multiple rewrites and changes. It has been said that the real skill in good writing lies in the writer's ability to edit, change, and rewrite.

Some copywriters feel most comfortable doing this through a series of sketch drafts, each one a little more complete and polished than the preceding one. Others prefer to revise as they go along, writing and polishing sentence after sentence until they have a relatively finished "first" draft. And, of course, other copywriters are somewhere between the two. There is no one right way. What's right for you is what works best.

Fortunately, in this age of computers and electronic word processing, change doesn't have to be quite as laborious as it used to be. This shouldn't reduce the number of rewrites, just make the process easier.

Whatever method you use to come to a final, completed draft, let's assume you have it in hand. Before going the next step—showing it to your client or internally for approval—let it sit for several days, perhaps even a week. Then run it through the following checks.

Check to See That Everything Is Covered. First, go back and review the objectives you established for the piece. Have they all been met? Next, review the outline. Has every important selling point and benefit been included? Then, ask these questions:

- Are the name of the company and product prominently and frequently mentioned?
- Do you get the essence of the story from the title, heads, subheads and illustrations?
- Are company experience and credentials discussed?
- Is every major benefit covered in a head?
- Are most minor benefits covered in subheads?
- Are major points reinforced with illustrations and captions?
- Is the product or service thoroughly explained?
- Is value or price addressed, either directly or by comparison to similar products?
- Is availability or dealer support addressed?
- Are enough specifications included to let the reader determine whether the product will fit his or her requirements?
- Have all references, specifications, and so forth, been checked for accuracy?
- Is after-the-sale service explained?
- Does the reader know what to do next?

Finally, check your copy against the literature of one or two major competing products. Does it cover the subject as well? Better? Is there any important point they have made that you forgot?

Check the Style. After checking for content, now check for communications ease, for copy readability, and for appropriateness to a specific reader—not the world at large. The following guidelines will help this process:

- Are there sufficient hooks to get the reader into the copy and keep him there?
- Is there one memorable theme or message that runs through the copy?

- Is a story presented with a beginning, a middle and an end?
- Is the story understandable?
- Is the story believable?
- Is the story compelling and enthusiastically told?
- Is the style appropriate to the typical reader?
- Is the information stated truthfully?
- Is the information stated persuasively?
- Can the copy be edited without substantially affecting style or information?
- Is the copy unique to the product, or could a competitor say the same thing?
- Does the copy flow easily from point to point?
- Does the copy lead you to action?

Finally, does the copy fit loosely within the guidelines laid down by the concept? If not, it should, or now is the time to revise the concept to fit the copy. If the copy has grown longer than originally intended, don't fret, provided it has been done well. Always keep in mind the following: *More people will read interesting long copy than undigestible short copy.*

Check It with Someone Else.   This is the final and in many ways the most important check. Every writer needs an editor.

Of course, in nearly all cases the copy will be reviewed and approved by the client before being printed. (For routing guidelines, see Appendix One.) But the client will probably not be a communications professional, so internal review—by another writer, the designer, an account person, a disinterested party— provides a last check for the copywriter to ensure that the copy is directed to the customer, not himself. This review will save the copywriter the potential embarrassment of having omitted the obvious, or committed the unpardonable.

TEN TESTS OF GOOD COPY

1. Good copy delivers a message in the heads.
2. Good copy has many visual breaks.

3. Good copy is engaging and reads fast.
4. Good copy is long enough to do the job, short enough to be interesting.
5. Good copy supports good visuals and vice versa.
6. Good copy has too many details to worry about one or two.
7. Good copy isn't excessively clever or cute.
8. Good copy sounds human and relates to the reader.
9. Good copy is unique, never interchangeable.
10. Good copy is persuasive and memorable.

CHAPTER 10

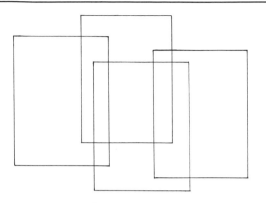

Layouts That Motivate: Guidelines for Judging the Role of Design in Literature

This chapter is generally about art, and specifically about layouts—the arrangement of visual elements in such a way as to both complement a written message and provide an independently powerful motivation for the literature reader.

For many of us, anything related with art is esoteric, and we are therefore hesitant to get involved in design issues or to criticize artwork. Unlike writing, in which we have all been schooled and which we employ every day of our lives, very few of us have had any real art training or experience, so we tend to "leave it to the experts."

For others, art is not nearly as complex as writing. It is simply a matter of deciding what we like or dislike. Words, after all, have to be at least read to be criticized, whereas art is immediately apparent to even the casual observer.

Both of these positions are gross oversimplifications. But both contain a strong element of truth, and they illustrate the reasons why there is so little rational criticism of literature design. Either it is not criticized adequately or it is criticized unfairly using arbitrary standards.

This chapter will provide some guidelines from which to judge the way art is employed in literature. It starts from the assumption that an individual's common sense, taste, and style are about half of what is required. Then it provides the other half, the basic information about the process of designing. Without that additional information, design can be a dauntingly complex and specialized field that is difficult to criticize intelligently.

The place to begin this process is by considering design as the architecture of the printed page. The designer employs various elements—shape, headlines, copy blocks, photos, and drawings—to build a communications structure much as the architect uses other elements to build a habitable structure. Then the designer uses type faces, paper, and color to finish the structure, to make it into a pleasant reading environment.

Just as a building must meet the structural criteria of being habitable and durable as well as being aesthetically pleasing, so, too, literature must meet two structural criteria: (1) it must independently communicate the ideas inherent in each of its sections and parts; (2) it must communicate totally as a unified, organic whole. When it meets these criteria in an aesthetically pleasing way, literature design organizes information better and focuses interest faster. It makes the ordinary interesting, turns the interesting into the extraordinary, and converts the important into the indelible. It ends up being more creative because it is more than creative.

With just a little background, anyone can evaluate how successful literature is in accomplishing these objectives.

THE SPECIALIZATION OF TALENT

The application of art and visual techniques to literature is a major part of a discipline called graphic design.

The title *graphic designer* is a relatively new one in the artistic professions, having been coined by American book designer William Addison Dwiggins in the 1920s. Previously, those who designed printed materials were simply called commercial artists, a title which most designers now consider very limiting but which is still heard frequently.

Because of the tremendous growth in the volume and variety of printed materials in recent times, graphic design is the fastest growing field of art. In addition to literature, graphic designers work on print advertisements, TV commercials, books, magazines, posters, trade show exhibits, and identification symbols (logos).

Graphic designers nearly always have specialized art training, some at the graduate level. They may work in an in-house design department, for a graphic design firm, for an advertising agency, or on their own on a free-lance basis. They may design literature exclusively, or they may perform other design tasks in addition to literature.

Obviously, the larger an organization, the more likely one is to find designers specializing in just literature, and the more likely one is to find different aspects of literature design being done by specialists. In smaller organizations it is likely that one person does most or all of the work, answering either to the title of art director, or designer. Even in smaller organizations, however, it is likely that at one time or another, one might find any one of the following titles used in a very specific way. It helps to know what each job describes and entails.

Art Director. This title is normally given to the senior design professional on a project; literally, the director of all art. The art director usually does all the conceptual thinking, any difficult visual problem solving, establishes design direction, and ensures continuity from design to design. Approval or modification of the final literature design before it is shown to the client is also the responsibility of the art director.

Designer. The designer on a project works out all the design details to the ideas and specifications of the art director. This may include the cover graphics, organization, pagination, type size and style, illustrations and photography, selection of paper, and use of color.

Mechanical artist. As the name implies, the basic function of the mechanical artist is the assembling of mechanicals. Because this operation requires pasting elements to "boards," the individual is also sometimes called a paste-up or board artist. Mechanical artists are either very specialized and meticulous craftspeople, or they are recently graduated graphic designers who are apprenticing.

Illustrator.   The illustrator takes an art director's idea and converts it into a drawing. Each illustrator has a distinctive style and usually concentrates within a certain area—for example, fashion, still life, people, technology, medicine, and so forth.

Photographer.   The photographer takes an art director's idea and converts it into a photograph. Although photographers' styles are not usually as distinctive as those of illustrators, each does have a "look" which makes him or her more or less appropriate for creating a given effect. Each photographer also has a reputation for providing a quantity of usable material within a given period of time. Most photographers also specialize, in fashion, portraits, industry, journalism, products, and so forth.

Others.   In addition, there are a number of other artistic talents which are regularly used in the preparation of art for literature. Most common are: calligraphers (hand-lettering artists), cartographers (mapmakers), cartoonists, and retouchers (of photographs).

FILLING THE BLANK SPACE

The page—this is where design begins and ends. It is something of a battleground where all the graphic action takes place: communications problem versus design solution.

Actually, the process usually starts much sooner. To a much greater extent than with writing, the broad concepts of design are often worked out before magic marker hits paper. Most designers have developed an approach (a style) which works well for them, are cognizant of design solutions worked out by other designers in similar situations, and are aware of design trends. Thus, while the entire process of design is highly intuitive and creative, much of what is done on paper is craftlike—working out the details with lots of trial and error.

It is this latter process that can be reviewed and impacted by another party. Here are some of the considerations that should go into the process of conceiving, assessing, rejecting, and accepting design solutions.

The Front Cover.   The combination of graphics, colors, papers, photos, folds, die cuts, logos, and type which can be used on the cover is infinite. So there is a natural tendency to overdesign covers. The best cover designs create a simple, appropriate and memorable first impression. They are clean, they are powerful, and they do more than decorate—they *communicate.*

Otherwise, the function of the cover is to be inviting and to entice an appropriate reader inside. Simultaneously, it must: (1) be in keeping with the style and character of the organization; (2) be at least in keeping with, and ideally illustrative of, the specific benefits of the product; (3) register the name of the organization and the product when appropriate. Don't settle for anything less.

The Inside Look.   Visual continuity is critically important for readability. It is carried by colors, typestyle, rules, and graphic devices from the front cover through each spread to the back cover.

The literature's overall feeling should be a contemporary one unless specifically designed for a "period" look. Readers generally relate best to what looks fresh, and they are equally turned off by the avant-garde and the passé. Remember, literature must be designed to work today, not yesterday or tomorrow. The only one who cares whether a design will still look fresh in 50 years is the designer who is trying to impress peers.

The literature's pages should have good proportions. They may be classically symmetrical or uniformly asymmetrical. It doesn't matter as long as each visual unit (what the eye sees at one time) is balanced.

The text and illustrations should be dramatized by the selective use of contrast: curved and linear forms juxtaposed, large photos near small, complementary colors playing off each other, convex versus concave forms. Use of the unusual provides visual breaks and dramatic effects.

The Grid.   A grid—a preset and consistently controlled breakup of page area—is simply a designer's way of organizing content and assuring continuity from page to page throughout the literature. It is particularly useful where large amounts of type or a number of diverse layout elements must be accommodated.

To arrive at a simple grid, margins for the page are first determined, then the page is split vertically into columns (3 is average for 8½ by 11 inch literature). After this, the page is split horizontally, so the effect is a grid of blocks, which can be numbered for convenience if necessary. The designer then arbitrarily decides how the layout elements will fall within this grid. Although this may suggest rigidity, a grid is actually nothing more than a loose framework for a structure which can be very flexible. Furthermore, a grid can be structured around any pattern of shapes. When it works as it should, a grid allows a sense of sequential continuity even when there is considerable variation in the content of each page unit.

It should be mentioned that the grid is the forerunner of a coming technology, as well. In the future, more and more design will be done by moving elements around on a video display terminal. Such computer-generated design programs operate on the electronic equivalent of a grid system.

The Copy Blocks.   These come in many forms; the simplest is single columns of running type, capped by a headline, and broken by occasional subheads with a lead-in sentence or statement. Sometimes a paragraph or two of highlighted type is used as an introduction, or summary. Or the material is set wider than the body text, a "deck" across the columns that follow it.

Copy blocks also include independent groupings of type. These include sidebars—mini-stories set outside the main body of text—as well as photo call-outs, captions, and footnotes, each of which is always read more than body text.

However set, it is the designer's responsibility to assure that copy blocks are balanced against themselves and other visual elements, and to ensure their readability. For copy blocks serve a dual function: as graphic elements that make the page inviting, and as holders of most of the literature's information.

Heads, by which we mean all titles or text leads, are also powerful graphic elements and copy summations. So they must be set to create interest and to pull the reader into the copy. *Above all, they must be easily read.*

Titles, headlines, subheads, and text leads should be graduated in visual impact—by size or by contrast—so that the reader quickly has a ranking of importance. They can be set in sizes larger than body text, or the same size but in bold or italic faces, or in contrasting type faces and colors. They should be as short as possible, especially if set in all caps. Using initial letters tends to make them difficult to read.

The best place for a headline—the major summation of a large block of copy—is at the top left of a page or spread, because the eye tends to read down and to the right. More importantly, the placement of headlines should be consistent, because a reader should be able to easily connect headline to headline throughout the piece to get a good summary of the literature's message.

The Illustrations.   Layouts work best when each visual unit (page or spread of two pages) has a dominant element which becomes noticeable at first glance and draws the eye into it. Although this can be a large headline or the arrangement of copy blocks, most often it is a graphic, a photograph, or other illustration.

It should be stated again here that the process of communications grows out of a blend of the pictorial and verbal. In good design, the two are inextricably intertwined and cannot be separated. In other words, the copy must support the visuals, and the visuals must support the copy.

Gratuitous illustrations with no reason or support—extra personnel shots, product photos, company real estate—have no place in well-designed literature.

Good layout depends upon simplicity; a key visual or strong grouping on each page or spread that sums up the message. The visual probably will work best if it has a single large mass and is relatively dark and dramatic. It should also have compelling interest and strong story appeal, the kind that immediately makes the reader ask, "what's going on there?"

Photographs can usually do this better than drawings because they are more lifelike. But sometimes photos don't fit within the style of the piece, or they can't make a point as strongly as an illustration or graphic.

A few things that help any graphic, illustration, or photograph are: a single, strong focal point; visual contrasts; vivid colors; dramatic lighting; and interesting people doing interesting things.

Products, particularly, should always be shown at their dramatic best, either in actual use by people, in exaggerated surroundings, or with "hero" lighting and staging. Moreover, it is important that all illustrations have a similar look. Use of illustrations made at other times for other purposes may be a little less costly, but it will probably be a lot less effective.

Finally, charts and graphs should be used sparingly to make a few important points. And each should be drawn so that it makes its point in one quick glance.

FITTING COPY AND SPECIFYING TYPE

It has been said many times that the best typography is that which is unseen. The typographic style with which a message is delivered should never interpose itself between the message and the reader. Typography is simply a means to an end: assured readability. So readability should be the only criterion for typographic excellence. Anything which is written to be read, should be able to be read—easily.

As self-evident as this might seem, good typography is not simple because of all the ways it affects how a message is read and absorbed. Typography can encourage readership, place emphasis, make words interesting, and grab the reader. Or it can make the reader stop reading.

In addition, legibility should never be confused with readability. That which is easy to read (legible), may not necessarily be inviting to read (readable).

Good typography is analogous to a speaker who makes a subject engaging, and thus transmits more information while making the information more memorable as well. As every good speaker knows, every speech, every audience, is different and has to be approached with different style and emphasis. This is also the case with typography.

An Evolving Art. There used to be lots of rules for typography. Some were dictated by tradition, but most grew out of the mechanical limitations of the equipment that set the type and the presses that printed from it. Today nearly anything is possible, so nearly anything is permissible.

For example, when all type characters were cast in metal and were assembled for letterpress printing in metal forms, a high degree of standardization was needed. Without it, nothing would fit or be repeatable from job to job. Now with computer-generated type and printing plates exposed directly from negatives, the same degree of precision is no longer necessary.

Today, type doesn't have to be set and spaced exactly the same way every time. Type faces can be electronically fattened, thinned, or distorted in nearly any conceivable way, almost instantaneously. Letters can be overlapped, too. And because electronics makes it much less costly to generate a new font (style) of type today, there are more choices available than ever before.

All this new freedom is not without its pitfalls, however. Now it is sometimes difficult to exactly match type when corrections or changes are made. Lines don't always appear parallel in printed material. Photographically blown-up heads are sometimes not sharp. Characters are sometimes butted or juxtaposed in ways that used to be impossible.

Without rules and mechanical constraints, there is also a temptation now for everyone to experiment, to throw all convention and rules to the wind. In the abstract, this is probably good, for it is only through experimentation that any art form advances. But experimentation always produces many more disasters than successes. Given the fact that we are considering typography for promotional literature which has to show a return on invested time and money, any desire to experiment should be carefully analyzed and justified.

In summary, now that we have the freedom to follow our typographic fancies, we must also assume the discipline to pursue only those few which look really promising.

Choosing the Faces.   The place to start any discussion of type-face selection is to recognize that there are two major groups of typefaces: *serif* and *sans serif.* As the names imply, one group has serifs—the ending strokes that give a character style—one group does not (serif faces are also often called "roman" faces). Each grouping has its proponents, especially when it comes to body text. Most designers, however, seem to favor sans serif faces, particularly when it comes to specifying type for promotional literature. Sans serif faces have been more fashionable since the 1920s.

Generally, sans serif faces are considered more modern; serif faces more traditional. Serif faces are generally thought to be more readable, because they seem to help the eye move from left to right. However, tests have indicated the sans serif faces can be just as readable in short lines. It is even possible to mix the two within one piece, but current wisdom has it that this should be done only as a contrast between headlines and body copy, or when the two are sufficiently separated, such as in a sidebar or box.

Within each group there are literally thousands of individual styles (faces). Each. will bring to a literature piece a slightly, or completely, different mood or feeling.

The bottom line on type face selection is simply that the choice is a highly personal decision which is also affected by the overall style of the literature. As long as the type is readable, there is no right or wrong, only personal taste.

The only other consideration in choosing the face is availability, and that is only a problem if you are restricted to one, limited, typesetting source.

Line Length and Spacing.   Typesetting is one of the few industries which has its own system of measurement. This system is not as universally adhered to as it was when typesetting was done only by members of the International Typographic Union, but it is still the accepted way. Not to understand its rudiments can severely limit one's ability to discuss type intelligently.

The system is built on points and picas. There are six picas to the inch, and 12 points to a pica (72 points to the inch). There are many other units of measure used (for example, see *agate* and *em quad* in the Glossary), but picas and points are all you really need to know.

Type size is always specified in points. Determination of size is made by measuring the distance between the tallest character's ascender (highest extension) and the bottom of its descender (lowest extension).

Distance between lines is called *leading,* from the thin strips of metal that were formerly used to separate them. It too is always specified in points. In fact, type and leading are usually specified together. For example, this paragraph is set in 11 on 13, meaning 11 point type on a 13 point base, or leading of 2 points between lines.

Line length is called the *measure* and is always specified in picas. The width of this page is 27 picas, or 4½ inches wide.

The right measure for readability is determined by type size, leading, and personal choice. As a rule of thumb, serif text is felt to be read most comfortably when there are about 10 words per line; sans serif text read most comfortably with about eight words per line. Another rule of thumb is that one and a half alphabets (39 characters) is the most comfortable measure for any given type font.

Type which is justified means that all lines are exactly the same length, with even right and left hand margins. Words are broken (hyphenated) and space is added between words (and sometimes letters) to make this possible.

Ragged type means lines of varying lengths, usually with the left margin constant and the right margin varying (although not always). The measure to which the type is set remains constant, but words are seldom broken and there is no word or letter spacing. Ragged right-hand margins are a fairly recent innovation, having been in use for about 50 years, and they are now preferred for most literature. There are two basic reasons for this: (1) ragged right-hand margins are thought to be more informal and "friendly" to the reader; (2) ragged right-hand margins are thought to be read faster than justified margins.

Two types of paragraph indention are commonly used. They are *regular indention* in which the first line of each paragraph is indented, and *hanging indention* where the first line of the first paragraph is set to full measure and the first line of each additional paragraph is indented. In addition, the term *flush indention* is used when there in no indention and paragraphs are separated with additional leading.

Making the Copy Fit.   Logically, the process is called copyfitting and it estimates the space typewritten copy will occupy when set in a particular type size and style. It is a necessary process to ensure that there isn't too much or too little copy for the total pages in the literature, or for a given space such as a caption block.

The process is actually quite simple. First the actual characters of the typewritten copy are counted. This is usually done by averaging the number of characters per typewritten line and multiplying by the number of lines. Next, using tables published by typesetters, the number of typeset characters per line is computed for a given type style, size, and line measure. Finally, the typewritten character total is divided by the number of characters per typeset line, which produces the number of lines required.

To find the depth that this number of lines will require, the depth of the individual line (its point size and leading), is now multiplied by the total number of lines. The result, in points, is the total column depth. To convert that figure to picas, divide by six; to inches divide by 72.

If the copy doesn't fit right—either too many words, or too few—the options are: (1) cut or add copy; (2) rewrite the copy to say the same thing in more or fewer words; (3) set the type in a size and style that takes more or less room; or (4) do a new layout with more or less space.

In addition, it should also be remembered that most foreign language text will take up more space than English. So if the text will require translation later, additional room should be available in the layout.

It is unfortunate that copyfitting is such a time-consuming and uncreative process, for it has led many designers to skip it entirely, preferring instead to guess at the amount of space the type will require. Although this is permissible in some jobs, it sometimes results in pages that end up crowded and in need of expensive resetting and editing to restore readability. Even more often it results in very open designs, purposely kept loose to ensure that the text will fit under any circumstances. This is usually at the expense of readability.

Within rather narrow limits, readability requires that there be a certain number of words within a designated space. Without copyfitting, it is impossible to know what this number is, or how the text will break. Simply put, precise copyfitting is an essential element in every good design.

Some Time-Tested Typesetting Conventions. Today there are few hard and fast rules for good typography. But these are typesetting conventions which are always worthy of consideration.

- Serif type faces are generally easier to read than sans serif type faces.
- Serif faces reversed out of dark backgrounds may plug up in printing, especially smaller type sizes. They should be avoided.
- Any text reversed out of a color background may plug up in printing, especially in smaller type sizes.
- Sans serif type needs more leading, and thus requires more room, than serif type.
- Boldface type needs more leading than the same size in normal weight.
- Long lines can be made more readable by adding leading.
- Text type will appear grayer as leading is added.
- Narrow columns (up to 10 words) normally don't require leading and can be set solid.
- Capital letters are more difficult to read than a mixture of capitals and lower case letters.
- Good text does not have "rivers" of space running through it.
- Good text does not have isolated words (*widows*) and lines (*orphans*).
- Crispness (edge sharpness) is important in overall text readability.
- Body type smaller than 8 point is difficult to read for many people.
- Body type larger than 12 point doesn't look like text should look.

CHOOSING THE RIGHT PAPER

Paper is one of civilized man's oldest and most enduring inventions; it has carried his written word for two millennia, his printed word for over 500 years. And, at least for the foreseeable future, it will continue to be the raw material from which all literature is produced.

Without paper we have, literally, nothing. It's obvious that for both aesthetic and production reasons, it is necessary to choose wisely the paper upon which the literature will be printed.

To do this, there are four general attributes of paper which must always be considered. We'll review them here in the most practical order, which is, unfortunately, the reverse of what's generally considered the ideal order of consideration.

Cost and Availability.   Paper has always been the most expensive single component in the preparation of most literature. In the past decade it has become even more so, because the increase in the cost of paper has far outpaced the increases in the cost of other literature elements.

Due primarily to environmental protection regulations and more expensive transportation, paper now runs from 25 percent of the literature's final cost on small jobs, to up to 35 percent on runs of several million copies. To ignore the cost of a particular paper is unconscionable.

It is the designer's role to select the paper which is the least expensive possible, consistent with the desired appearance and printing quality. Because supplying paper is a highly competitive business, it is often possible to get an alternative paper with appearance and printability similar to the first choice at substantial savings.

Availability must also be considered when selecting paper. Commonly used papers are normally stocked by paper distributors or printers in sufficient quantities for all but the largest literature requirements. Very large quantities of paper usually require a special run at the paper mill and this can take several weeks or months, depending upon the mill's scheduling. Likewise, specialty papers, even in small quantities, are not always stocked by paper distributors; they must be ordered from the mill's stock or made specially. In either case, this can mean the difference between meeting or not meeting a printing deadline.

Size and Weight. Today most printed material is produced several pages at a time on sheets (or continuously on a web) which are then folded, bound together, and trimmed to a final, often common, size. Therefore, for efficiency, paper is produced in standard sizes which work best in standard size production machinery (presses, folders, etc.).

These paper sizes are important design considerations because the cost of wasted paper and extra production time to produce an odd-sized literature piece is such that it can substantially increase the bill. Any literature of non-standard size, or with special folds or die cuts, must always be reviewed in light of how much added impact the added cost will justify.

Paper weight (sometimes referred to as its basis or substance) is also an important consideration because it gives a general indication of how thick or bulky the literature will be. In addition, paper weight considerably affects mailing and distribution costs. And, as might be expected, lighter weight papers cost less than heavier papers of the same quality.

The designer's goal is often to get the lightest weight paper that has all the other necessary characteristics—appearance, color, opacity, texture, and ink acceptance.

The weight of a given kind of paper is determined by an arcane system which weighs 500 sheets of a standard size. Unfortunately, each general kind of paper (there are about a dozen) uses a different size as its standard. Thus, 22 pound writing paper is substantially lighter than a 22 pound book paper.

One simplifying factor in this confusing scheme is that most literature is produced on paper for which the standard size is 25 inches by 38 inches. This means that any 22-pound, or basis 22 paper, is of such density that 500 sheets of it will weigh 22 pounds.

Papers used in literature for text run from 50 pound (quite thin) to 100-pound (quite heavy). Cover papers, which are nearly twice as bulky as text papers per given weight, are normally used which have a weight running from 40 pound (light) to 90 pound (heavy).

Runnability.   Whether or not the designer oversees the printing will affect whether he or she can be held responsible for printing quality. The designer is, however, always held responsible for the runnability of the paper.

Runnability refers to the proclivity of the paper to go easily through the production process, and to easily produce a desired effect. Papers with bad runnability take longer on press, don't perform consistently, and often cause delays in the finishing operations. There are two major factors which must be considered in determining runnability. Both have to be weighed in relation to cost and availability and are usually learned only through trial and error. It is for this reason that many designers are reluctant to try a new paper or a new printer, especially when faced with a tight deadline or a fussy client.

First and most important is the effect of ink on the paper; more specifically, the way a particular printer puts particular inks on a particular paper. Generally, the rougher the surface the more ink will be absorbed, and the duller and less sharp the type and illustrations will appear. Conversely, the smoother the surface the more ink will be "held out" on the surface, and the sharper, more brilliant and dense everything will appear. For these reasons, most literature which contains halftone illustrations or color is produced on papers which have a surface coated for smoothness and ink holdout.

The second major factor to consider is the way the paper handles. The paper will probably have to be folded and cut, and perhaps even diecut, embossed, or stamped. Each of these (and other) processes is affected by the paper's characteristics.

For example, papers which have been calendared and given a heavy "cast" coating for maximum ink holdout tend to crack along the folds unless extra care is taken to score them prior to folding. Lightweight papers tend to rip or pucker when diecut. Papers with a textured surface tend to emboss irregularly. And the direction of the paper's grain will affect the sharpness of the folds.

Appearance.   There are thousands of different kinds of paper. Each is slightly different from its closest kin. And each has physical characteristics that affect the reader's psychological reaction to the message being presented. Even after limitations of cost, availability, and runnability are considered, the choices are still almost limitless. In the end this makes the paper selection a subjective choice, subject to the following guidelines:

The paper (or papers) used in any literature piece should match the mood of the message being conveyed. Some papers are more lively, some more subdued, some more elegant, than others.

Paper color and brightness can affect the way images are reproduced, noted, and remembered. Type will probably be more readable on a soft, off-white surface. Halftones will be more attractive and contain more detail when printed on a hard, white surface in which artificial brighteners have been incorporated for extra "snap." Shiny surfaces usually make text more difficult to read, but enhance halftone appearance. Other considerations are:

- When paper is to be printed on both sides, opacity can be a critical factor.
- The effect of color inks on color papers may not be totally predictable.
- Some typestyles seem to reproduce better on some papers than on others.

PRESENTING THE IDEA

How many great ideas have been lost because of a bad presentation? Probably no more in the design world than in any other. But given the fact that design is both a visual discipline and a means of communication, it shouldn't happen here at all.

It is important that design ideas be effectively presented to assure that reason and logic will be available to counter the inevitable subjectivity with which they will be reviewed. Too many designers fail to remember that good ideas alone are never enough. Or they adopt the simplistic arrogance that good ideas are all that matters.

As in any other commercial endeavor, *the ability to communicate the validity of ideas (to "sell" them) is every bit as important as the ideas themselves.* In design, this means assuring that layouts are complete enough to be easily understood. And it means explaining as necessary the translation from layout to the actual printed piece.

A layout will later serve as an important guide to production, but its first and most important function is to provide an indication of what the client can expect to see in the printed piece. Therefore, it must be as accurate a representation of future reality *as required.* The more finished the representation becomes, however, the more expensive it becomes, so it should never be any more than required. This means that in each individual case a designer must be sensitive to how much layout detail is enough and how much is too much. Doing so is every bit as indicative of solid professionalism as is the sophistication of the designs produced.

Generally, layouts can be done in one of three levels of tightness, or detail. Occasionally all three are used as a concept is refined and it proceeds through increasingly important approval levels.

Thumbnails.   These are the least detailed layouts, usually used to assure agreement before going farther. They are small sketches of page spreads, normally an inch or two high, although sometimes larger. They are laid down sequentially on a board. They show number of pages, use of color, columns, and illustration placement. However, because no headlines or text are rendered, they don't indicate story content or readability. And because they are miniatures, there is no feeling of paper bulk or texture.

Sketches.   This is the way most layouts are presented most of the time. Sketches are normally done to scale, either *1:1* (full size) or *1:2* (half size). They are loosely rendered but allow one to judge the relationship of type to visuals and to preview the kind of graphics that will be used and the content of any illustrations. Headlines are lettered in and copy length is shown. Sketches are often presented in book format so the actual feeling of page turning is duplicated.

Comprehensives (Comps).   These are the most detailed layouts. They attempt to capture the actual feeling of the printed piece for a particularly important or difficult presentation. Usually, the layout is *1:1* (full size) on the actual paper on which the piece will be printed. The cover is completely rendered. Headlines are set or lettered in the actual type face to be used. Copy is shown in its appropriate length in "greek," or even set. Cropped and sized color prints are pasted in the place where they will be reproduced.

Whichever type of layout is used, it should always be presented to the client by the designer. While it is tempting for the designer to simply send the layout, or to assign its presentation to someone else, the person paying the bill deserves, and should demand, more.

Only the designer can explain the rationale of the layout completely and can discuss the possible changes which will affect the design's integrity. Further, direct feedback from the client usually results in a better end product because of the creative interaction that's part of the review process.

Finally, layouts should always be presented with copy, so that the latter can be evaluated in the context of the design, and vice versa. (See Appendix One for guidelines on how to ensure efficient review of material within an organization.)

LOOKING INTO THE (AUTOMATED) FUTURE

Ultimately, only three things are really important in literature design: that the quality is good, that the work is produced on time, and that the cost is within budget.

That's easily said, but until very recently it took a heavy dose of talent and years of accumulated craftsmanship to accomplish—no longer. Things have changed, and are continuing to change, rapidly.

Computer-aided design is now quickly reducing the absolute necessity of human craftsmanship. Like it or not, in many instances it is now far faster and easier (albeit not necessarily less expensive) to let a computer handle many of the routine functions of graphic design. Moreover, when done by computer, the results are nearly always more accurate and reliable than when done by hand.

In addition, often the process of conceptualizing can be done better and more economically at a computer workstation. The more design experience and skill that is applied the better the result will be, but for many less complex jobs they are no longer absolutely necessary.

The products that make all this possible are loosely called computer graphics, or electronic media systems. They are basically nothing more than a set of time-proven design tools adapted to electronics. Although technologically complex and expensive ($50,000 to $325,000 at this writing), if computer graphics systems follow the pattern of other electronic innovations, we can expect to see prices drop in the future.

To use a computer graphics system, the designer simply sits before a blank screen with an electronic pencil and tablet rather than at a drawing board with paper and felt-tipped pen.

The designer first selects from a menu of choices. The computer provides the ability to paste-in photographs and illustrations, do freehand drawing, paint sections of the screen with an unlimited selection of colors, set headline type, establish blocks for copy, and draw rules.

Once put on the screen, all of these elements can be quickly and easily moved about, changed, and resized as necessary until the pages look just the way the designer wants.

Then, with a few commands to the computer, the results can be printed out on conventional or photographic paper for review or approval. Or the results can be imaged directly to photographic film to be used as reproduction art.

The big advantage of such systems is that they relegate to the computer that which it can do fastest and best (moving, pasting, sizing, and drafting), and thus free the human mind to do what it does best (conceptualizing, creating, and experimenting). In short, by accelerating or eliminating most of the everyday unproductive work that has nothing to do with creativity, computer graphics systems actually enhance creativity.

It is, of course, to be expected that this new technology—like all others before it—will be resisted, even when it becomes easily affordable. It threatens the insecure.

But computer graphics and media systems are part of the future, particularly for much routine literature design. Smart designers will see them for what they are—nothing more than better tools that can be used to implement and expand the imagination.

TEN TESTS OF A GOOD LAYOUT

1. A good layout mirrors the style of the organization it represents.

2. A good layout complements the product.
3. A good layout helps the reader identify what's important.
4. A good layout gives headline statements visual impact.
5. A good layout has readable text.
6. A good layout has interesting illustrations that sustain reader interest.
7. A good layout uses graphics to explain and inform, not merely to decorate.
8. A good layout looks stylish and up-to-date.
9. A good layout never looks crowded or busy.
10. A good layout is different enough to make the literature memorable.

Photo courtesy of Lightspeed Inc.

Figure 10–1. Computer graphics workstations such as this one are revolutionizing the way much literature design is done. Using a variety of electronic tools, a designer can conceptualize, create, and experiment much faster than ever before possible. That's because a computer does all the tedious work such as moving, pasting, sizing, and drafting.

CHAPTER 11

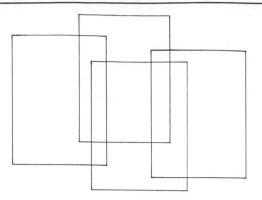

Production: Understanding Purchasing, Scheduling, Printing, and Finishing

The importance a reader will place on a particular literature piece is directly related to how he or she first perceives it. If the piece appears to be important it will be considered important, and vice versa.

Chapters 9 and 10 are devoted to two of the determinants of importance: writing and design. Now, we consider the third determinant: production, the actual process of getting the writing and design onto paper. What happens in the production process will strongly affect the overall look and feel of the piece, how it reads, and the appeal of the design and illustrations.

The effect of even the best written and best designed piece can be enhanced or diminished tremendously by the procedures employed in production.

An understanding of these procedures—what goes on after all the creative work has been done and approved—is necessary to purchasing production services effectively, and criticizing production results with credibility.

As used here, the word *production* refers to more than the

act of printing, or putting ink on paper. It includes all the procedures involved, from typesetting to binding. Nonetheless, in dealing with production we are primarily dealing with the printing industry and, like any manufacturing industry, it is a business built around specifications.

We now leave the realm of the subjective and move into more objective territory. The art of production does involve many subjective judgments, but it mainly employs a series of mechanical processes which are pretty straightforward, at least in their primary forms.

THE LENGTHY PROCEDURE

Does it have to take so long? That question is probably heard more than any other by those who sell production services. No matter how complex or simple the job, it always seems to take too much time. Once all the creative work has been done and approved, everyone is anxious to have and to use the literature. So every literature piece always takes longer in the production cycle than its originators anticipated. The average for most pieces is four to six weeks.

One reason for the anxiety is simply the modern obsession with instant gratification. The pressures of business add another dimension. And last but not least is a lack of understanding of all that's involved.

Producing most literature pieces involves highly complex procedures, highly trained craftspeople, and highly sophisticated equipment. Moreover, the efficiency and economics of the printing industry dictate that each job be meshed with a number of others running concurrently.

The production time for quality work will probably always be measured in weeks, despite the tremendous strides being made in speeding up the process. Twenty years ago it averaged nearly twice as long as today for high quality work.

Understanding what is involved in each of the five steps of the production process will help in determining where time can be cut from any particular job with the least effect on quality.

Type and Mechanicals.   This is nearly always the designer's responsibility, but it is nonetheless a part of the production process. The aesthetics of type are covered in the previous chapter, so here we will address only the production considerations: obtaining the type and arranging it in the page formats (mechanicals) which the printer needs to proceed.

Modern typography can be done by hand from individual letters, cast by a machine in metal, produced by typewriters and other impact printers, or assembled from preprinted and stick-down letters (transfer type). However, most high quality type today is produced photographically on paper or film by computers.

Depending upon the number of words and how many different type sizes and measures are involved, the text for most literature pieces can be keyboarded (typed), set, proofed, and delivered in three or four working days by even the most meticulous typographer. Corrections can usually be made overnight.

Given the fact that very sophisticated computers are employed, there are only two things that prevent the type from being produced even faster: the hand operation of keyboarding each character into the computer; and the typographer's need to schedule work flow. The latter is subject to negotiation. The former can be reduced considerably if the text is produced on a word processing computer and that electronic information fed directly to the typesetting computer.

Once set, the type is sent to a mechanical artist in the form of paper reproduction proofs known as galleys—long strips of paper with the type produced as unbroken columns. Headlines and subheads are normally produced on separate galleys from the text, or at the beginning or end of a text galley. The mechanical artist takes the galleys, cuts them apart, and assembles the type in a page mechanical along with rules, graphics, illustrations, and windows for photographs. This can take up to several hours per page, per artist. In estimating mechanicals for a 6-page booklet, figure about one man-day; a 12-page booklet, about two man-days; a 24-page booklet, about four man-days. Normally the only way to compress this time is to have more than one artist working on the mechanicals simultaneously, but that greatly increases the chances of inconsistencies and errors.

It should be mentioned here that all of these procedures are subject to rapid change caused by the emergence of electronic page composition systems. Although too expensive at this writing for most literature production, they are already widely used by newspapers and magazines. For more information, see "electronic printing" below.

Halftones and Separations. Any illustration with varying tonal values, such as most photographs and paintings, must be broken down into a collection of small dots of various sizes for printing. This is because most printing processes produce only solid color, so any tonal values must be created through optical illusion. The bigger the dots, the blacker that area of the illustration appears to the eye; the smaller the dots, the grayer.

When thus screened, illustrations are called halftones. They can be made in varying degrees of fineness, determined by the number of dots in a linear inch. The coarser the printing paper and the less concern about reproduction quality, the coarser the screen used. The finer the printing paper and the more concern about quality, the finer the screen. Also, it takes a lot more time and skill to print fine-screen halftones than it does coarse-screen halftones.

For coarser paper, such as newsprint, a coarse 65 lines-per-inch screen is used; for the very finest papers and printing, a 300 lines-per-inch screen is used. Most literature uses 150- to 200-line screens, which produce excellent quality without excessive time and care.

Making a single black-and-white halftone for printing—rephotographing the illustration to break it into dots—takes approximately one-half hour. It is not a step which normally presents an opportunity to save on time or costs.

Making a color halftone, however, is considerably more complex. It involves an additional step called separating, the process of breaking the illustration down into the three primary colors—cyan, magenta, and yellow—which, along with black, are used to produce full-color printing.

To produce a set of separations for each illustration (they usually take the form of negative films) involves a series of interrelated judgments regarding color values, properties of the printing inks to be used, idiosyncracies of the printing press, and paper characteristics.

Once made, the separations must be proofed, then hand-manipulated and hand-corrected, often many times, until they produce a result close to the original. This laborious and time-consuming process is called *color correction*. Because of the time and hand effort, producing good color separations is one of the most expensive steps of the production process.

Making color separations is also possible on an electronic device known as a color scanner. It not only takes a lot of the subjectivity out of the process, it also makes it faster. The problem is, basic scanners cost about $250,000, complete color-scanning and page makeup systems cost up to $1 million. Thus, the price of separations remains high whether done by hand or machine. However, scanners have been one of the reasons why color separations can be done so much faster today than a decade ago, and why there is so much more good color printing.

To do 10 color separations for a brochure averages about a week in most facilities. To try and reduce this time is to seriously risk jeopardizing color quality. If you find that much more time than this is scheduled, it is probably due to the desire of the company making the separations to smooth out workflow.

Printing. Literature can be printed by any of the printing processes described later in this chapter. But today it is mainly done by offset lithography on one of two different types of presses: sheet-fed and web.

Sheet-fed presses print single sheets of paper containing many pages, one sheet at a time. They allow printing on the widest variety of papers in the widest range of sizes. They also permit exacting quality control. They are, however, considerably slower for large quantities than are web presses. Typically, high-quality sheet-fed printing takes place at about 6,000 impressions (sheets) per hour.

The size of the press (e.g., 25 by 38) indicates the *maximum* size sheet (in inches) the press will accept. The number of colors (e.g., a two color press) indicates the number of colors that can be printed in *one pass* of a sheet. For example, if a four-color job is run on a two-color press, the sheet has to be passed through twice. The press will print on one side only, unless it is a perfecting press, which indicates the ability to print both sides more or less simultaneously.

Generally, the bigger the press and the more colors it can

print at one pass, the more pages it will print at once and the higher the charges will be for its time. Also, the longer in advance the printer will try and schedule it and the less flexible that scheduling will be. In a more positive vein, the larger the press, and the more pages and colors it can print at once, the faster the job can be printed.

Web presses print on a continuous roll of paper which is then cut (and usually folded) automatically at the end of the press. Web presses nearly always print four or more colors, on both sides, in one pass. They are very limited in terms of sizes that can be printed economically, they require large runs to be cost-competitive, and they must be tightly scheduled long in advance. But they can print the right job many, many times faster than sheet-fed presses. (Web press speed is measured in feet-per-minute (fpm) printed; typical speeds are around 1,000 fpm.) If a long run can be anticipated far enough in advance, web printing can substantially reduce press time and costs.

As an illustration of actual press time: 25,000 copies of a 9 by 12-inch, 12-page, four color brochure will average from three to five press days on a sheet-fed press; about one-half day on a web press.

Why is it then that up to twice this amount of time is normally indicated in a production schedule? For the same reason that airlines overbook; not everyone shows up when he is supposed to.

Even a relatively small (25 by 38 inch) two-color press costs the printer several hundred dollars an hour in overhead, and most printers have several presses, some much larger. Thus, every hour a press is unoccupied represents a tremendous financial drain. The only way to minimize this is to overbook and to provide as much scheduling flexibility as possible so that jobs can be moved around, from press to press and from day to day, as necessary to keep everything flowing smoothly and economically.

Keeping this in mind, there are two things a printing customer can do to assure the fastest possible printing time: (1) notify the printer far in advance so he can reserve press time and have paper available; (2) absolutely guarantee (through some type of financial penalty for nonperformance) that you will meet whatever schedule the printer determines. If these conditions are met, the time normally allocated for most printing can be cut by up to half.

Finishing.   After the pages are printed, they must be assembled and finished in the final literature format. Since many pages are printed (ganged) on a few sheets of paper, this process involves folding and trimming at the very least, and it usually involves collating (assembling) and stapling. In addition, other work may be required such as scoring or perforating, embossing or engraving (raised letters or shapes), die cutting (irregular-shaped cutouts), laminating (applying a high gloss finish), and imprinting.

The part of the printing plant in which all this is apt to happen is called *the bindery*. Most printers have such facilities to fold, score, staple, and trim what they print, and larger printers also often include the ability to imprint and laminate. But nearly all printers employ the services of trade binderies to do such specialized work as embossing, debossing, die cutting, silk screening, stitching, gold stamping, or binding hardcover books.

When only folding, collating, stapling, and trimming are required, bindery time averages about half as long as four-color printing time on a sheet-fed press, or 25 percent as long as two-color printing on a sheet-fed press. However, if specialized in-house bindery work is involved, such as laminating, another day can be added. And if the work has to be sent out to a trade bindery, as would be the case for die cutting, at least two additional days need to be added to the schedule.

THE MAJOR PRINTING PROCESSES

There are several printing processes available to put words and illustrations on paper. Each was invented or evolved to provide economy in particular situations or to solve a particular set of production problems. Regardless of the process, each more or less employs the production procedures outlined above.

Each printing process requires: (1) that all illustrations be broken down into dots of varying size so that solid ink can give the illusion of tonal gradation; and (2) the layering of transparent color inks (normally four—cyan, yellow, magenta, and black) to provide the illusion of true color reproduction.

The differences between the various ways of printing aren't normally important to getting better literature produced more economically. In any case, most of today's literature is printed by just one of these processes, offset lithography. It is important, however, to know at least the principal advantages and disadvantages of the five major printing methods.

Letterpress.   This is the process most people think of when they think of printing. In its simplest form, it employs a block (a piece of type, or an engraving) on which there are two surface levels, one raised (in relief) relative to the other. Ink is spread on the raised surface and the block is then pressed (hence the word press) in direct contact with the paper. The result is that everything on the raised surface that has been inked and contacts the paper, prints. Everything on the lower surface that does not get inked and does not contact the paper, does not print. This simple process has been in use for thousands of years.

The big breakthrough came in 1450 when Johannes Gutenberg developed a system which allowed the use of individual letter characters which could be assembled as desired, then disassembled for use again in another page. This invention of movable type speeded up the printing of text by doing away with the need to laboriously hand engrave each page from a block of wood or metal.

For over 500 years, letterpress was the most prevalent method of putting ink on paper and it set most commercial printing standards. There is, however, a severe limitation to letterpress printing which has recently led to a rapid decline in its popularity.

To make a letterpress printing form takes either the labor-intensive assembling of many different pieces of metal—type, halftone blocks, rules, etc.—or the expense of engraving all these elements onto a single metal block. And when printing, it is difficult to keep all the form elements at exactly the same height so the printing is uniform across the page, and from page to page, without considerable care and expense.

Because of these expenses, letterpress is used today primarily for newspaper and magazine printing which require very long runs at very high speeds; the plates used can be extremely durable. In addition, letterpress is often preferred for the printing of type on soft papers because of the distinctive look which it produces.

As for printing literature, letterpress is used mostly for the imprinting of a changeable line or two (for example, a dealer or agent name) on small quantities of a large run. It is also used occasionally to impart its rich aesthetic quality to pieces which are completely or mainly type.

Gravure.   This method of printing (technically, intaglio) is exactly the opposite of letterpress because it employs a plate with sunken wells which hold the ink. Just before the paper comes into contact with the plate, its surface is automatically wiped clean, leaving only the ink in the wells to be transferred through direct impression and capillary action to the paper.

The shape to be printed is engraved into the plate, producing the well which holds the ink. The depth of the well, which can be varied, determines how much ink will be held, and subsequently how much ink will be transferred to the paper. Thus, it is possible for illustrations to have not only the tonal gradation produced by varying dot sizes, but also the additional dimension of varying ink thicknesses. For this reason, and because gravure inks are necessarily very fluid, they produce soft and rich photographic reproductions which appear almost screenless. Gravure reproductions also vary considerably less across a press run because of the toughness of the plates. And, finally, gravure allows fine reproductions on a much cheaper grade of paper than is possible with either letterpress or lithography.

Another intaglio process, called engraving, is sometimes used to produce extra crisp typography and extraordinarily fine lines. It is not suitable for reproducing photographs and requires special, soft paper. To see an example, you need look no farther than your wallet; for counterfeit protection, engraving is the method used to print nearly all currency and negotiable securities. Engraving is also used for high-quality invitations, letterheads, and business cards.

The biggest drawback of gravure for literature printing is the very high cost of making the plates from which the printing is done. Also, type printed by gravure is never crisp and sharp. Therefore, it is used for literature printing only when its particular advantages are paramount, when the run length is in the neighborhood of half a million copies, when photography plays a dominant role, and when type is sparse and at least 12 points or larger.

Engraving is sometimes used to produce literature with a special effect or to simulate the look of a high quality invitation.

Lithography.   Letterpress prints from raised surfaces, gravure from depressed surfaces, and lithography from flat surfaces. Moreover, while the aforementioned processes are purely mechanical, lithography is a mix of the mechanical and the chemical.

Because it is dependent on chemical technology, lithography has been slower to develop than the other processes. Lithography played a minor role in the printing of literature as recently as World War II. Now, however, it is by far the dominant process because it provides tremendous flexibility and economy.

Basically, lithography relies upon the tendency of oil and water to repel each other. Through photographic or mechanical means, the image to be printed is applied to a specially-prepared flat surface. This surface has a natural affinity for water, which means it also has a natural repulsion for grease. On the other hand, the image area is produced so that it attracts such greasy substances as printing ink. Before paper touches it the plate is rolled with a water-charged roller, immediately followed by an ink-charged roller. The ink is repelled from the background area and sticks to the image area, where it waits to be transferred to the paper.

This process was invented in 1798, and for about a hundred years relied on the use of flat limestones as the printing "plate" and greasy pens as the imaging source. It became, and still is, a favorite medium for artists. As a commercial process, lithography became increasingly popular as flexible metal plates replaced cumbersome stones, as photographic imaging became possible, and as new inks, papers, wetting solutions, and presses were developed. Because the new metal lithographic plates were much less costly than letterpress or gravure plates, the more plates needed to print a job—a function of the number of pages and number of colors—the more cost-efficient lithography became.

The use of thin, flat metal plates makes lithography particularly well adapted to offset printing. This is a technique in which the ink is transferred to another surface, such as a rubber cylinder, before it is finally transferred to the paper. This additional step provides even greater printing control and higher quality. Today very little pure lithography is done, and practically none is done in the printing of literature. Rather it is nearly all offset lithography now, and that has resulted in the whole process being referred to as "offset."

Silk Screen. This process is highly specialized and is considerably different from the others, because it does not use a plate to print; instead printing is done from a stencil.

The stencil is an actual screen of silk or other porous material on which certain areas have been blocked out. Ink is forced through the screen in the image areas and is held back in the nonimage areas.

Although silk screen printing has an advantage over other types of stencil printing because it is not necessary to connect freestanding areas (such as the center of an "o"), it does have most of a stencil's limitations. These include very slow printing speeds, the inability to produce small type, and difficulty in producing halftone illustrations.

However, silk screens are relatively inexpensive to prepare and can be used to print on odd shapes and delicate surfaces; the classic example is the surface of an egg. The process is generally used for small runs of large items, such as posters, or for the printing of fabrics. In literature production, it is also used occasionally for printing a graphic or a single line of type for an unusual effect.

Electronic Printing. This is the printing of the future, rapidly evolving and showing more promise every year. It combines data processing, image scanning, and xerographic technologies.

With electronic printing, words are typed into a word processing computer where they are automatically converted to a type style and size, and put into a page format. Images (photographs, artwork, etc.) are electronically scanned with a TV-cameralike device and also fed to the computer where they are screened, sized, cropped, and retouched. Both type and images are then displayed full size on a video terminal for arranging and formatting at will—including changing type style and size, line lengths, and halftone size.

When the page has been proofed and looks exactly the way it should, it is then electronically transmitted to a laser printer, close by or hundreds of miles away, where a xerographic plate is automatically exposed by laser beam. Printing and collating then takes place at speeds of up to 6,000 sheets per hour.

The quality is somewhat limited: printed pages have an appearance similar to that of Xerox copies. And only line art and coarse-screen halftones can be produced at this time. It is not possible to print four-color illustrations at present, and even two color reproduction is rare. Finally, the possible sheet size, which determines the number of pages which can be printed at once, is small.

Despite these limitations, electronic printing is ideal for the publication of many instruction books, catalogs, and other material which is printed in small quantities. Other materials which are mostly text, and which need to be constantly revised and updated are also suitable for electronic printing. As the technology develops and quality improves, it should find increasing applications in the production of other types of literature as well. In many cases it will allow clerical personnel to supplant the traditional functions of the designer, typesetter, and printer.

PURCHASING EFFECTIVELY

Printing is one of the world's largest industries. In the United States alone, several billion dollars are spent each year on all types of printing, and a significant portion of that expense is for the materials we have labeled promotional literature. Indeed, when packages, books, magazines, and newspapers are subtracted from the total, most printing revenue comes from literature.

Because a large sum of money is usually involved, and because the expected result can never be totally quantified, the purchasing of printing must be very carefully controlled. Even a small organization can spend hundreds of thousands of dollars a year on printed literature, and large organizations can spend millions. At the very least expenditures should be coordinated, and at best the purchasing function should be centralized under competent supervision.

Unfortunately, the buying of printing too often lacks either control. It is often handled either by someone unskilled in purchasing procedures, or by a purchasing agent unskilled in the uniqueness of the printing processes. Having a purchasing procedure is important, but it is also important to recognize that the procedure must be different from that used to purchase other business items. Although specifications and timetables are also involved, there is still a substantial element of subjectivity and interpretation which is missing from other purchasing activities.

It is not the purpose of this text to provide a primer on the purchasing of printing. Rather, what is presented below will provide a few simple rules that can act as a checklist to assure that the proper procedures are always carried out.

In addition, most printers follow industry standard trade customs which specify certain responsibilities regarding delivery and ownership of preparation materials. Anyone purchasing printing should be familiar with them. They are reproduced in Appendix Two.

Are the Specifications Exact? No matter what the printed piece is, no matter how simple or complex, the buying procedures will be less exact than those employed in purchasing nearly any other item commonly found in business.

Precisely because there are so many facets of printing that cannot be rigidly specified, it pays to be as specific as possible about those that can be. At a very minimum, make sure the following details are provided the printer, along with a copy of the layout, marked up to show color breaks.

- Quantity. Specify the number of copies which must be printed, as well as the quantity desired.
- Size and number of pages. Specify the final size, the number of pages (including cover), and whether there are any

fold-out pages, laminations or special bindery considerations.
* Type of paper. Specify it by mill, brand name, and weight.
* Cover. Specify whether the same stock is used for the cover as the text, or if it is different. Also, is there any additional finishing necessary on the cover such as embossing, die cuts, or pockets?
* Number of colors. Specify if the job is to be black and white, four-color process, or some mix of special colors. Also, is a varnish finish required on any of the sheets?
* Halftones. Specify whether the originals are prints or transparencies, and give their sizes. Indicate if any need special work. Make separate lists of black and white, duotone, and color halftone reproductions, and give their printed sizes as well as screen ruling desired. Indicate if any halftones bleed off the page.
* Delivery. Specify a date desired, and indicate if that date is inviolable, as would be the case if the literature is needed for a one-time event. Also, specify where the literature is to be delivered.

Have the Right Printers Been Considered? More than in most businesses, every printer is different from every other printer. Some are highly specialized and accept only certain types of printing, such as publication and financial printing. Even within the broad classification known as commercial (or sometimes advertising) printing there is great variation.

Some commercial printers want to do only short run work, some want only very long runs. Some thrive on difficult challenges, others want only the routine. Some are highly skilled in one type of printing, but mediocre in others. Specialties and standards vary enormously. It all depends upon the printer's particular blend of experience, equipment, and personnel.

In addition, even a competent printer who has experience, equipment, and personnel to handle a particular type of work may not want to accept a job if his capacity in that area is overbooked. He may be looking for a different type of work.

For all these reasons, it is good to have a stable of printers from which to choose. Also, because printing is a highly subjective craft in which personal attention to detail is so important, it is wise to build relationships through repeat business. Finally, since shipping costs can be a significant percentage of a printing bill, it is always better to use a local printer, if all other factors are equal.

Have Competitive Bids Been Obtained?   The first-time purchaser of printing is always shocked by the wide disparity in prices quoted on the same job from otherwise reputable and seemingly competitive firms. Differences of 30 percent or more are not uncommon. Does this mean there is no market consensus on what printing should cost? Yes: that is, not in the sense of most competitive businesses. The reason is simply that a given printer's pricing on a particular job is almost wholly dependent on a unique set of conditions in effect at the time a quote is given. There are, literally, hundreds of factors that can change that quote on a weekly basis. What is expensive one week may be inexpensive the next due to the sudden availability of future press time (idle presses cost money), the need to take up slack in the color separation department, or the ability to print your job with something similar.

In short, the prices any printer quotes on a given job can vary enormously from week to week. For this reason, whenever possible the purchaser of printing should always price-shop among printers of equal capabilities and reputation.

Unlike the creative aspects of literature preparation where bids and quotes can often be self-defeating, such bids are necessary and expected when printing is purchased. From specifications similar to those listed above, it is standard procedure to obtain at least three written quotes from printers qualified to handle the job.

Was the Final Selection Made on a Basis Other than Price?   It is important to obtain at least three quotes to provide both a cost guideline, and to require the printer to go through the exercise of assuring that he has made his procedures the most cost efficient possible. It does not follow, however, that the printer with the lowest bid has to be selected. Some purchasers usually select the middle of the three bidders. Others go with a favorite, as long as his bid is not more than 15 percent more, and so forth.

The point is that price should never be the sole criterion for selection. There are so many subjective elements in the printing production process, and so many things that can go wrong, that selecting a printer based only on low price can end up being more costly. It is far better to select a printer based on reputation, quality, and service, and to use the quote as a way of assuring that this capability is being purchased competitively.

Finally, it is worth noting that the large sums involved, coupled with the imprecision of selection criteria, provide fertile ground for graft. For this reason, *it should be a standard organizational policy that a selection made on any basis other than price be justified briefly in writing and entered as part of the permanent job record.* Along the same lines, the acceptance of lavish entertainment or gifts with a value of more than $50 should be expressly forbidden to anyone with purchasing responsibility.

ENSURING THE JOB GETS DONE RIGHT

Producing all but the very smallest literature pieces is usually a time-consuming, complex procedure that involves dozens of individuals at both the client and printer levels. The result is that hundreds of things can go wrong.

Keeping mistakes to a minimum and assuring that everything flows smoothly and efficiently takes two things: (1) rigidly followed schedules; and (2) clearly assigned responsibilities.

Scheduling. The actual production schedule will be determined by the printer according to the client's needs and the anticipated receipt of the materials needed for production. However, if these materials (mechanicals, artwork, etc.) are delayed, the schedule will quickly become meaningless. Therefore, preproduction or creative, scheduling is usually more important than scheduling the production steps that follow it. Too often the production schedule, a professionally prepared and binding agreement, is completely invalidated by an amateurish arrangement of what precedes it.

A valid preproduction schedule requires a detailed list of the steps the job requires, who is responsible for each of these steps, and *the name of the one individual who has the responsibility to assure that each step is completed on time.* Without this, it will be virtually impossible to produce a complex job in a reasonable time frame, especially in an organization where a number of jobs are proceeding simultaneously.

Although most schedules can easily be kept on a sheet of paper, or a simple printed form, there are also now a number of microcomputer software scheduling programs which simplify the process.

Responsibility.   Both prior to and during production, one person should be responsible at the client level for assuring that all steps are completed on time, flagging any possible problems, and routing materials to appropriate personnel. In addition, *one* person should have responsibility for signing off on each of the following:

- Final review of the mechanicals should be the responsibility of the *copywriter,* after approval by the art director. This will provide a check against all the things that can negatively affect readability in the translation from typewritten text to composed page. These include inappropriate text juxtapositions, bad word and paragraph breaks, obscure head and subhead statements, and overwritten captions.
- Final review of blueprints (or brownlines or saltprints) should be done by the *project manager,* after approval by the art director and copywriter. Because they are proofs folded to size with all text and illustrative elements in place, blueprints provide a good approximation (without paper and color) of how the job will actually appear. They are also the last chance to check for mistakes (such as "flopped" captions) before plates are made and the job put on press. Although correcting mistakes at the blueprint stage is more expensive than earlier, it is much less expensive than after plates are made and the job is on press. Specifically, blueprints should be checked to assure that: there are no missing elements; all photographs and captions are in the right places; the piece folds correctly;

the page numbers are correct; there are no spots or blemishes.

- Final review of color proofs of the photographs is the responsibility of the *art director* (or in large organizations, by a production coordinator) who should look for: fidelity to the originals; overall color balance; smoothness of retouching; registration of the color plates.
- Final review of the press sheets is the responsibility of the *art director* (or in large organizations, by a production coordinator) who should look for: a match to the color proofs; reproduction sharpness: ink lay; inking consistency across the sheet and from sheet to sheet; paper printability.

TEN WAYS TO CONTROL PRODUCTION COSTS

1. Keep current on new technology—word processing systems, electronic design stations, page makeup systems, laser printers—and use them whenever practical.
2. Set type from *final*, approved copy. Then read the mechanicals for typos and errors. Use the blueprints or brownlines only to check for printer mistakes.
3. Spend money on good artwork, so you can save money on retouching and color correction.
4. Remember that designs which call for special printing or finishing techniques—unusual inks, die-cuts, fold-out or pop-up pages, embossing or debossing, laminates, scoring, etc.—cost more to produce. Sometimes it is worth the extra cost, sometimes not.
5. Be aware of the seasons when commercial printers in your locality are unusually busy (such as when annual reports are being printed), and avoid trying to print literature during these times.
6. Obtain bids only from quality printers with a demonstrated capability to handle work similar to what you have planned.

7. Provide the bidding printers with exact, detailed specifications.
8. Use the bidding process only to assure cost-efficiency and competitiveness, not necessarily for selection.
9. Allow the printer to schedule the job at his convenience whenever possible.
10. Hold the job until it can be run at the same time (ganged) with another job having similar specifications, if you can.

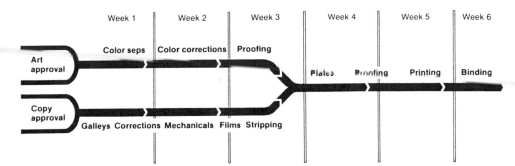

FIGURE 11–1. A typical production timeline for the printing of 25,000 16-page (self cover), four-color brochures.

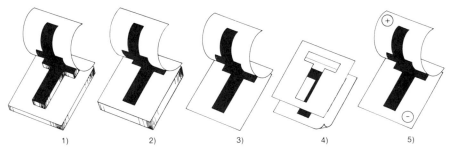

FIGURE 11–2. A simple view of the five major printing processes. Shown left to right are: (1) letterpress, or printing from raised surfaces; (2) gravure, or printing from depressed surfaces; (3) lithography, or printing from chemically treated flat surfaces; (4) silk screen, or printing through stencils; (5) electronic printing, or printing from electrically-charged flat surfaces.

XQ4 - Request for Quotation

To Mail in Window Envelope Fold at Guide Marks.

Purchasing Department
The Typical Company
1234 Any Street
Any City, Any State 00000

REQUEST FOR QUOTATION

NUMBER	DATE
241	11/24/86

THE ABOVE NUMBER MUST APPEAR ON ALL
QUOTATIONS AND RELATED CORRESPONDENCE
THIS IS NOT AN ORDER

DATE DELIVERY REQUIRED	REPLY NOT LATER THAN	REQUISITION NO	JOB NO	
2/19/87	12/1/86	a865932	S874	Mr. A. Buyer

VENDOR

.Able Press
.Franklin Drive
.Any City, Any State 00000

$ 27,052
65.98 M

.Best Press
.Best Industrial Park
.Any City, Any State 00000

$ 38,335
93.50 M

.Competitive Printing
.Circle Road
.Any City, Any State 00000

$ 31,995
78.04 M

SUMMARY OF QUOTATIONS

ITEM	QUANTITY	VENDOR NO. 1	VENDOR NO. 2	VENDOR NO. 3

TERMS
F.O.B.
DELIVERY

TERMS	2 F.O.B.	3 SHIPMENT VIA	4 SHIPPING WEIGHT	5 DATE SHIPMENT CAN BE MADE
net 30	Any city	your option		

ITEM	QUANTITY	DESCRIPTION	6 UNIT PRICE	7 AMOUNT
1	300M 10M 100M	"Thor" sales literature English language French language Spanish language		

Number of pages: 8   plus cover -- self cover
Bleed: no
Finished size: 5 3/8 x 7 3/8"
Flat size: 21 1/4 x 7 3/8"
Inks: 4 colors + gloss varnish 2 sides
Stock: 80 lb L.O.E.G.T.
Composition: supplied
Mechanicals: supplied
Separations: supplied
Proofing: Cromalin and salt
Binding and finishing: trim and fold to size as per dummy
Packing: shrink wrap in 500's
Schedule needed: yes
Delivery location: 867 Typical Drive, Any City
Special instructions: supply prices on reprint w/no change
                      based on same quantities
Production supervision: J. Smith, Typical
Questions: call A. Buyer 999-9999

ORDER PLACED WITH _____*Able*_____

P.O. NO _a865932_ DATE _12/8/86._   BUYER _A Buyer._

REASON ORDER PLACED WITH SUCCESSFUL VENDOR

LOWEST PRICE	QUALITY	BEST DELY	SERVICE	ONLY SOURCE	BEST DESIGN	OTHER REASONS
☒	☒	☐	☐	☐	☐	

FIGURE 11–3. Prices quoted for a given job will have a wide disparity among printers of the same capability, depending upon the particular set of conditions in effect at the time the quote is given. For this reason, three competitive quotes should always be obtained. Shown here is a standard request for quotation form. A copy was sent to each of the three vendors shown. On each of these copies the names of the other vendors don't reproduce, so each vendor has no idea who he is competing with. When the quotes were received they were transcribed to the original form, a decision made, and the original entered as part of the permanent job record.

Photo courtesy Interleaf, Inc.

FIGURE 11–4. Electronic printing systems allow type to be set and pages to be formatted right on a video terminal such as the one shown here. When everything looks exactly the way it should, the page is electronically transferred to a xerographic printer which prints and collates at speeds up to 6,000 sheets per hour. It is the future for much short-run printing.

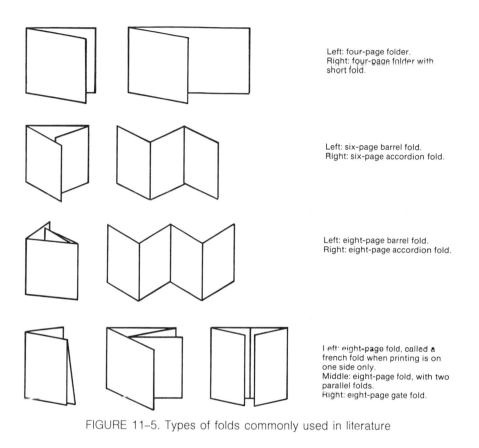

Left: four-page folder.
Right: four-page folder with short fold.

Left: six-page barrel fold.
Right: six-page accordion fold.

Left: eight-page barrel fold.
Right: eight-page accordion fold.

Left: eight-page fold, called a french fold when printing is on one side only.
Middle: eight-page fold, with two parallel folds.
Right: eight-page gate fold.

FIGURE 11–5. Types of folds commonly used in literature

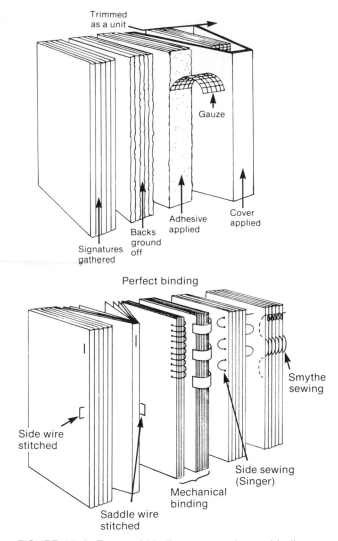

Perfect binding

FIGURE 11–6. Types of binding commonly used in literature

CHAPTER 12

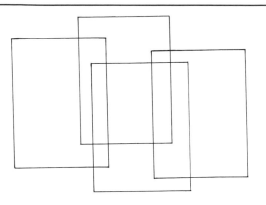

Distribution: Getting Literature to the Reader

The previous chapters of this section have described ways in which the skill of preparation can make promotional literature more appealing, readable, informative, and convincing. In short, ways it can be made more effective for the purpose intended.

To this we must now add one final, mostly overlooked but overriding, consideration: the way in which the literature finds, or loses, its way to the appropriate reader. At worst, what happens in the process we call distribution can make all the foregoing meaningless. At best, it can only assure that what should happen, actually does.

As in any communications process, all the skill in the world is to no avail when there is no audience. Distribution is the way literature finds an audience. It is to literature what circulation is to print ads, what rating points are to commercials, what lists are to mailings, what locations are to sales promotions.

THE NEED FOR A STRATEGY

In recent decades, while each communication medium and vehicle has become more refined, there has also been a strong trend toward coordinating and integrating communications with other marketing activities. More companies now think in terms of total marketing strategies, more agencies now bill themselves as total marketing organizations.

Integrative marketing is in vogue and as a strategy it makes lots of sense. By coordinating various communications and other marketing activities so they can complement and enhance each other, a significant multiplier effect is attained. As stated earlier, however, the process usually doesn't include literature. Even when it does, too often a lack of attention to distribution dilutes the effort.

Frequently the scenario goes something like this: the sales force hits the road on a sell-in blitz; dealer orders are taken and the product is shipped; commercials hit the air, ads appear in national magazines; dealers run coop tie-ins in local newspapers. And in come the customers.

But the product dies at the counter. Perhaps because dealers weren't informed about sales features; or because the product was hard for customers to understand; or because it appeared too expensive; or because the manufacturer was unknown. Each of these problems, and many not mentioned, could have been addressed by literature availability.

A similar scenario could be constructed in business-to-business or industrial marketing around all the "requests for information" which go unanswered, and which result in customers who go unsold.

Maybe somewhere in the integrative marketing strategy sessions someone forgot that nonimpulse-sale products usually need literature help. It is more likely that the need was recognized but there was just no strategy for distribution, or no plan to ensure that the strategy was carried out.

WAYS TO IMPROVE CIRCULATION

No matter what the literature type, there are two principal ways for it to reach its intended audience: through direct circulation by the producer, or through the efforts of a second party such as a dealer or agent. Before considering these two ways, however, we should also note the obvious: *The single best way to improve circulation is to make the literature desirable.* This is true regardless of whether direct or indirect methods are used. Obtaining efficient circulation of literature that is unappreciated and unwanted is many times harder than for desirable literature.

A literature program with a history of producing timely, attractive, and informative pieces goes a long way toward assuring this level of desirability. Unfortunately, even this is seldom enough by itself. In addition, some type of merchandising help is usually necessary.

It should be a standard element of a company's literature program to try and enhance the value and expand the circulation of its literature. This can be done through a conscientious effort to include literature in ads, offer it in house organs, promote its use through dealer bulletins, and announce its availability in internal newsletters.

If sound merchandising techniques are applied to literature that is already well produced, all that remains to be done is to assure that the distribution system will provide as much efficient circulation as possible.

Direct Distribution. This takes place when the prospect is handed the literature, receives it in response to a request, or gets it through the mail. You directly control how and when the distribution takes place, and any problems—real or perceived—reflect directly on your organization and its products and services.

As even the most junior salesperson knows, nothing turns off a prospect faster than ignoring a specific request. Nevertheless, each year millions of specific requests for literature—solicited at trade shows, promised by sales representatives, offered through magazine "bingo" cards, and generated by other literature and mailings—go unacknowledged. Such lack of action is not only lamentable rudeness, it's also stupid marketing.

No offer should ever be made without the mechanism and the appropriate literature to fulfill the request. All this normally takes is the management sophistication and foresight to assure proper coordination and control of the offering to media and individuals.

Make sure literature will be stocked in sufficient quantities before any offering is made. Make sure that bingo numbers don't appear on ads if there is no literature, or the cost of offering it outweigh the benefits. Don't place "request for more information" cards in literature unless there is something *additionally* meaningful and useful to send, and so forth.

When you do fulfill, act quickly—within a week or two. Send the literature in an attractive envelope, ideally with a printed notice that says that requested material is enclosed. Attach a pleasant, informative transmittal letter or form that thanks the prospect and provides information on what to do next. Printed forms are perfectly OK; a personal reply isn't necessary. But what is necessary is both the courtesy of a thanks for expressing interest and an honest desire to keep the communications process alive until the prospect decides to shut it off.

Effective direct distribution also takes advantage of new, inexpensive ways to increase circulation and amortize costs over a larger base. Literature can be offered in print ads, broadcast commercials, and house organs. Capability brochures and annual reports can be mailed to all employees as a way of keeping them informed and loyal. There should be an automatic procedure to add names and to delete them from house-organ mailing lists. Instruction booklets and introductory brochures should be sent to field sales representatives and dealer salespersons as a way of familiarizing them with a new product.

In short, there are numerous opportunities for increasing direct distribution effectiveness. The usual limitation is only a lack of attention to the possibilities.

Dealer or Agent Distribution.   This second, indirect, method of literature distribution is obviously less controllable. But, there are things that can be done. For example, part of a sales representative's evaluation could address how effectively literature is employed. The sales representative should maintain dealer inventories and encourage dealers to use literature for in-store merchandising; and the sales representative should use it on sales calls.

Dealers and agents, as well as company sales representatives, often have to be reminded of the tremendous power promotional literature can have. Getting the right literature into the right hands at the right time shortens the sales cycle, sells more products faster, and generates more profit. This can be accomplished by "talking-up" the use of literature and by placing articles on new literature releases in dealer bulletins and newsletters. The importance of literature can be further highlighted by soliciting, and heeding, comments on how to make it better.

Also, make sure that your literature is easy to order. Provide a semiannual illustrated catalog that lists what is available. Include a postage-paid, self-addressed order card. And ship all orders promptly.

Help the dealer with in-store merchandising using literature. Decorate product displays with it. Provide counter cards with a pocket to assure that the literature stays organized on the counter near the product. Make self-standing plastic racks available to allow it to be displayed neatly in nearly any counter location. And when lots of literature is available, a wall display rack provides attractive promotional decor while organizing a lot of useful information for customers.

WAYS TO KEEP COSTS IN LINE

Most of the above suggestions will raise literature costs while increasing effectiveness and generating more profit. So a literature distribution plan has to be budgeted and its short-term costs have to be justified in terms of long-term communications effectiveness.

These are some ways of making existing distribution practices more efficient and offsetting any additional costs.

- Stop distributing large amounts of literature automatically. Provide reps, dealers, and agents with starter quantities. Then, make sure the literature is easy to order, and ensure that it is requested. Always ship it to an individual's attention.
- Consider charging dealers and agents, and cross-charging within an organization. Establish and publicize *share-cost* literature unit prices which represent some fraction of actual production costs (25 percent or so). This adds value to literature and reduces waste; the amount charged is

small enough that there will be few serious objections. What few objections there are can be covered by amending coop reimbursement plans to cover literature. Don't look at this as a way of recouping costs, though, as most of the revenue generated will be eaten up by the increased administrative expense.

- Be more judicious about what literature is given out where. Screen requests for house organs. Never allow expensive brochures to be placed on the sales counter. Minimize or do away with literature at trade shows; see if isn't better to bring a few sample copies in a display binder, along with many literature request forms. This will reduce waste and assure the requester that the literature will be sent directly to his place of business where it can be more thoughtfully read. As a bonus you get another name for your mailing list.

TEN WAYS TO ENSURE AVAILABILITY

1. Make sure literature is included on all marketing strategy checklists.
2. Make sure distribution time is included on all literature production schedules.
3. Put a code number on the back of every piece so you can tell at a glance when it was produced, in what quantity, and with what authority.
4. Build a permanent file of all information pertinent to the literature, and key that to the code number on the piece. This will allow you to easily determine all information relevant to approvals, printing, and distribution, and will speed up reprinting and redistribution.
5. Restrict literature inventory to a few locations, preferably one distribution center. This will help reduce the quantity required for "pipeline filling," and will guard against the continued use of obsolete literature.

6. Inventory literature at least once a year, as you would products. Make sure at this time that no obsolete literature is available for distribution.
7. Maintain an ordering and inventory system for literature as you would for products. The more sophisticated and automated the system, the better.
8. To the extent possible, keep a record of who uses literature at what times. This is valuable not only for maintaining adequate and up-to-date inventory, it also provides more sources for information on effectiveness.
9. Keep a separate inventory, perhaps held by a printer, of pieces that are to be imprinted. It may help to have the literature stored as flat sheets, unfolded. Also, try to arrange to have ordering, imprinting and shipping handled separately from other literature orders, so as not to bog down the regular distribution system.
10. Keep an inviolable master library of two or three copies of each literature piece for historical, creative, and legal purposes.

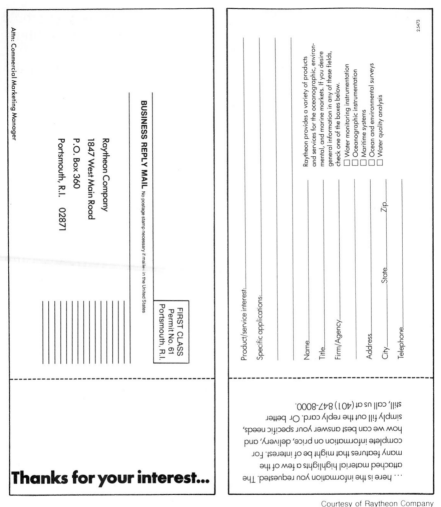

Courtesy of Raytheon Company

FIGURE 12–1. A simple, preprinted literature transmittal form that thanks the recipient while providing a way to request additional information. The top folds over the literature being sent.

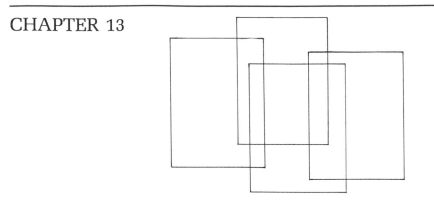

CHAPTER 13

A Perfect Example

Presented here is a perfect example of promotional literature—perfect because it follows all the rules that result in literature effectiveness. Whether the piece itself actually is perfect, of course, is another matter and not relevant. For in literature preparation, perfection should always be considered as a process, not a state.

In any event, this small brochure prepared by Apple Computer provides an illustration of several points made in the preceding chapters. In that sense it provides a summary of the points made previously, albeit an incomplete one.

The fact that this is a small brochure, that it is printed in color, that it is about computers, and that it was designed for store distribution is irrelevant. All the factors that make this piece work so well are equally appropriate to other forms of literature, in color or black-and-white, for other markets, with other forms of distribution.

Here's why this literature works so well.

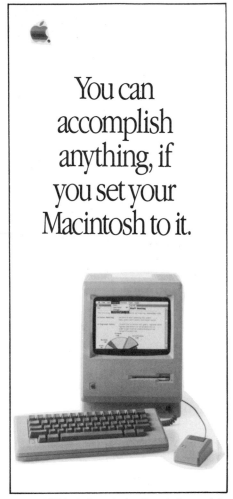

Front cover

- The dimensions of 3⅞" by 8½", are perfect for rack display on a sales counter and to fit into a customer's inside jacket pocket or purse. Also the unfolded sheet size of 17" by 14¾" reduces paper waste because it can be printed in multiples on a standard-size paper.
- The title statement attracts interest, is flattering to the reader, and conveys a strong product benefit: ample power to address any job.
- The product name is prominently mentioned.
- The product is prominently shown.
- The company is identified.

First fold

- The headline appeals to readers' interests while conveying a product benefit—versatility.
- The body copy is well written and tells an interesting story.
- An informal typeface is set for easy readability.
- Graphics tell a story independent of copy.
- The layout reinforces that versatile doesn't mean complicated.
- Concise summary statements are used.

Second fold

- Another headline that states a product benefit—quality—in readers' terms.
- Body copy backs up the challenge in the headline.
- Good copy detail for credibility.
- Graphics provide information as well as decoration.
- Concise summary statements are used.

Give it everything we've got.

Macintosh comes ready to start doing everything you need to do.

And it's ready to keep growing with you.

The basic system includes the computer itself, with its built-in display and disk drive. A detached keyboard. And the mouse.

You get a tutorial—the "Guided Tour of Macintosh" disk and audiocassette. And a

The Macintosh External Disk Drive lets you store and retrieve more information—quickly and conveniently.

manual that sets new standards for ease of use in computer manuals.

Then, when it's time to expand, there's an expansive array of options.

If you want to store more information—and get to it faster—think about an additional disk drive for your Macintosh. The Macintosh External Disk Drive adds a second high-capacity 3½-inch disk drive—like the one already built into your Macintosh.

If that's not enough, you can add a Macintosh Hard Disk 20 to your system, putting 20 megabytes of storage capacity at your fingertips. Hard disks with a variety of configurations are also available from other companies. The Hyperdrive internal hard disk, for example, lets you store all the information and programs you need, right inside your Macintosh.

You can get to the whole world fast when you put it at your fingertips with the Apple Personal Modem. Together with a telephone and a communications program such as MacTerminal, the modem lets your Macintosh communicate with other computers and tap into electronic information services.

Add a modem, such as the Apple® Personal Modem, to your Macintosh, and you can share information with other computers. And with MacTerminal™ software and AppleLine,™ Macintosh can even share the power of an IBM mainframe, by emulating a 3278 terminal.

You can also choose from a variety of printers—for print quality ranging from slightly better than the crisp, clear text and graphics you see on the Macintosh screen to better than you ever dared imagine.

The Apple ImageWriter II is the ideal printer when you have just one Macintosh—or want one printer per Macintosh. It's a dot-matrix printer with the power to reproduce everything you see on the Macintosh screen: Sharp, clear type in a variety of styles and sizes. Finely detailed graphics. Proportional text. And mixed text and graphics.

When you're in a hurry, the ImageWriter II can skip the fancy stuff and turn out a quick draft. Its new optional sheet feeder makes it even more convenient.

For traditional-looking business correspondence, Macintosh also works with letter-quality printers made by a number of other companies. (Letter-quality printers produce text that looks as if it's been typewritten.)

And when you want to look absolutely, unquestionably, authoritatively professional, look at the LaserWriter.

It's like having an art department and typesetter at your desk. Because now every piece of paper your business produces can have the official feel and eye appeal of published documents. From the simplest memo to the most important presentation for the board of directors.

The versatile ImageWriter II prints finely detailed graphics, and prints text in a variety of typefaces, styles, and sizes.

The LaserWriter comes with built-in typefaces—for example, Times™ and Helvetica,™ two of the most popular typefaces in the world.

All can be printed in a variety of styles, such as bold and italic. And in sizes limited only by the size of the paper.

The LaserWriter also prints full-page graphics. And prints both text and graphics on the same page—at the same incredibly high resolution.

It prints on many types of paper, too. From your company's letterhead to plain copier paper.

In letter, legal, and international sizes. On transparencies. And on labels and envelopes.

The LaserWriter can quickly earn its keep. Especially when you consider the printing and graphics bills you won't be paying anymore.

What's more, up to 31 Macintosh computers can share a LaserWriter over the AppleTalk™ Personal Network, making it even more cost-effective.

Other companies make a number of products that you can share over AppleTalk, such as shared storage devices. There are also products that let you connect IBM PCs and other networks, such as Ethernet, to the AppleTalk network.

To sum up, Macintosh comes well equipped. Right out of the box, it's ready to do more than you ever thought a personal computer could do.

So you can do more than you ever thought you could do, better than you ever thought you could do it.

Which means when you need to give it everything you've got, give it everything we've got.

A Macintosh personal computer system.

You see, while some people have worried about keeping up with technology, at Apple we've concerned ourselves with something much more important.

Because the way we see it, it's technology that hasn't been able to keep up with you.

Until now, that is.

The LaserWriter can create professional-looking printouts of virtually anything you can put on a Macintosh screen.

After all, you've always been able to think faster than you could write. To manage system could manage your workflow. To see more than you could show.

You've always been better than your tools.

Now, finally, there are tools that let you think, work, and look as smart as you really are.

Which will make some people nervous. And some people Macintosh owners.

Macintosh comes with a built-in display and disk drive, a separate keyboard, and the mouse. You can expand your system with an expansive array of options. And with hundreds of business programs, such as Microsoft Excel (shown here).

The Macintosh Hard Disk 20 gives you fast access to more than 10,000 pages of information. So you can store application programs, along with all your files, in one convenient place.

When you need to crunch numbers, use the Apple Numeric Keypad to make fast work of spreadsheet, accounting, and other number-intensive projects.

Third fold

- This page, like others, is designed and written to be read either independently, or as part of the rest of the brochure.
- Interesting double entendre headline.
- Call-outs are used for detail that would slow down readership of text.
- Accessories are described in terms of benefits they offer to the reader.
- Concise summary statements are used.

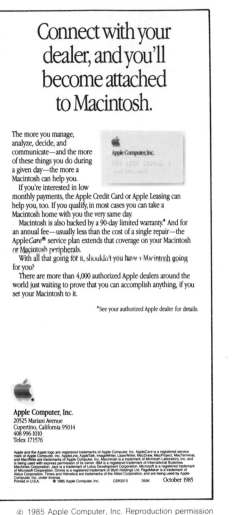

Connect with your dealer, and you'll become attached to Macintosh.

The more you manage, analyze, decide, and communicate—and the more of these things you do during a given day—the more a Macintosh can help you.

If you're interested in low monthly payments, the Apple Credit Card or Apple Leasing can help you, too. If you qualify, in most cases you can take a Macintosh home with you the very same day.

Macintosh is also backed by a 90-day limited warranty.* And for an annual fee—usually less than the cost of a single repair—the Apple*Care*® service plan extends that coverage on your Macintosh or Macintosh peripherals.

With all that going for it, shouldn't you have a Macintosh going for you?

There are more than 4,000 authorized Apple dealers around the world just waiting to prove that you can accomplish anything, if you set your Macintosh to it.

*See your authorized Apple dealer for details.

Apple Computer, Inc.
20525 Mariani Avenue
Cupertino, California 95014
408-996-1010
Telex 171576

Apple and the Apple logo are registered trademarks of Apple Computer, Inc. AppleCare is a registered service mark of Apple Computer, Inc. AppleLine, AppleTalk, ImageWriter, LaserWriter, MacDraw, MacProject, MacTerminal, and MacWrite are trademarks of Apple Computer, Inc. Macintosh is a trademark of McIntosh Laboratory, Inc. and is being used with express permission of its owner. IBM is a registered trademark of International Business Machines Corporation. Jazz is a trademark of Lotus Development Corporation. Microsoft is a registered trademark of Microsoft Corporation. Omnis is a registered trademark of Blyth Holdings Ltd. PageMaker is a trademark of Aldus Corporation. Times and Helvetica are trademarks of the Allied Corporation, and are being used by Apple Computer, Inc. under license.
Printed in U.S.A.   © 1985 Apple Computer, Inc.   CSR3313   350K   October 1985

Back cover

- The headline encourages dealer loyalty.
- Why every reader can afford the product is explained.
- Warranty and service concerns are answered.
- A call to action is included.
- Room is left for dealer imprint.
- Distribution and printing information is included for internal control.

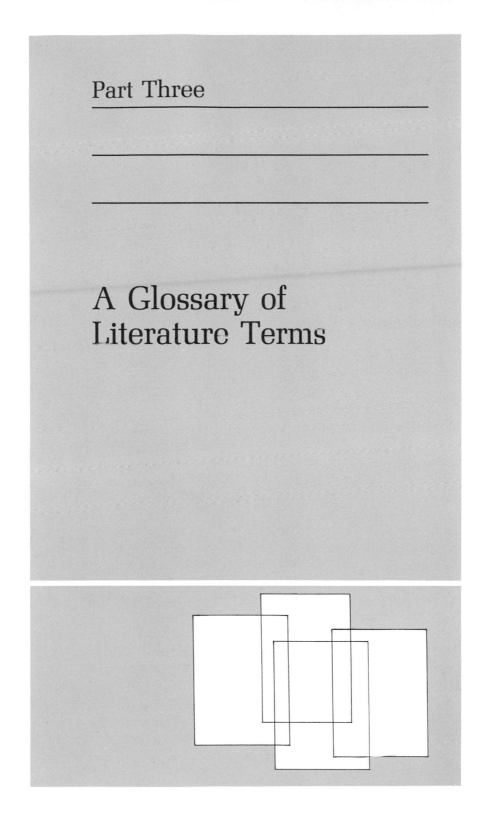

Part Three

A Glossary of Literature Terms

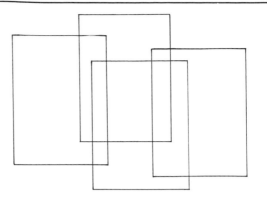

Terms Used in Literature Preparation

a.a.   Printer's or proofreader's abbreviation for author's alteration.

Accordion Fold.   Two or more parallel folds of paper which open like an accordion.

Advertising.   The purchasing of publicly-available space or time for the purpose of presenting a message.

Agate Line.   A newspaper unit of measurement, occasionally used for literature. 14 agate lines equal 1 inch.

AIDA.   A popular copywriting formula, especially for direct response media. It stands for: get Attention, arouse Interest, stimulate Desire, ask for Action.

Air.   Designer's slang for the white space within a *layout*.

Annual Report.   A report to shareholders required of all publicly held companies by the Securities and Exchange Commission.

Art.   Generally, any drawing or illustration in literature. May also be used to refer to the *layout*.

Artwork.   See *art*.

Backing Up.   Printing the reverse side of a sheet already printed on one side.

Basis.   The weight of paper. See also *substance*.

Benefits.   The satisfactions a reader will get from certain product attributes. Usually, the reasons for purchasing. Contrast to *features*.

Bindery.   That section of the printing plant where finishing—cutting, *binding*, packaging and shipping—is done.

Binding.   The method by which literature pages are fastened together. Also, the final finishing step of the printing process.

Bingo Card.   A postage-paid reply card bound into a magazine on which there are numbers keyed to advertisements. The reader who wants more information circles the appropriate numbers and mails in the card. The magazine then distributes the requests to the appropriate advertisers for fulfillment—usually literature.

Bleed.   Any printed matter that extends to the very edges of the page with no margins.

Blueprints.   A photoprint on blueprint-type paper made from the films which will be used to expose the printing plates. It provides a final check for the client before the job goes on press. See also *brownlines* and *saltprints*.

Boards.   See *mechanical*.

Body Type.   Text type, usually from 6 to 12 points.

Brochure.   Multi-page literature, usually 4 inches by 6 inches or larger.

Broadside.   A sheet of printed information used as a handout. See also *flyer*.

Brownline.   The same as a blueprint, but made on a paper which has a brown tone.

Bulk.   Paper sheet thickness, or the thickness of the literature piece.

Camera-ready.   Any material ready for reproduction.

Campaign.   Any promotion done on a regular basis with a common theme or elements.

Capability Brochure.   Literature designed to tell the story of an organization rather than specific products or services.

Catalog.   A booklet describing products and their prices and availability.

Chrome.   A photographic transparency.

Circulation.   The actual number of copies of any item actually sold or distributed. Does not include samples or waste.

Clip Art.   Prepared black-and-white illustrations on a variety of subjects which can be clipped and pasted into a mechanical.

Collateral.   Stictly, literature that is tied directly to another medium, such as a *brochure* offered in an ad; literature that does not have a life of its own. Often used erroneously to describe all literature.

Comprehensive. A detailed rendering of what the literature will look like when actually printed.

Composition. Material set in *type,* or the setting of *type.*

Composing Room. Place where *type* is set.

Concept. The central idea, or theme, of the literature. Usually presented in rough sketch form with headlines.

Continuous Tone. A photograph or other illustration which has a range of tones between black and white. Cannot be printed without screening. Contrast to *halftone.*

Controlled Circulation. A term which describes *house magazines, newsletters,* etc., which are provided free to a specific group.

Co-op Money. Reimbursement by the manufacturer for part or all the costs of promoting a specific product at a specific time. Often applied to literature.

Copy. A manuscript; the words in any literature piece.

Copyfitting. The process of determining the amount of space necessary to accommodate typeset *copy.*

Copywriter. A person who prepares written material, usually for commercial purposes.

Cost-per-contact. Total costs divided by the number of persons reached. See also *Efficiency.*

CPM. Cost per thousand. A measurement of *efficiency.*

Crop Marks. Thin black lines placed at the corners of the *mechanical* and printed on the press sheet that show the exact dimensions of the page.

Cropping. Eliminating part of a photograph or illustration to make it fit a space or be more effective.

Cut. Any illustration.

Deboss. Any shape that is depressed (sunken) into a paper's surface. See also *emboss* and *die.*

Demographics. Statistics about people, their occupations, incomes, education, etc. Often the basis for determining the quality of an audience.

Die. A specially made steel knife that cuts or *embosses* or *debosses* an irregular shape into paper. See *die cut,* below.

Die Cut. Any irregular shape or design that requires cutting with a *die.*

Direct Mail. Any promotion using the mail as a transmittal medium.

Direct Response.   Any mailing or ad which solicits an order or other response.

Double-dot Duotone.   A way of producing a black-and-white illustration with an extended tonal range through the use of two different *halftone* negatives.

Duotone.   A printed illustration consisting of two colors.

Efficiency.   Any quantitative determination of how well one item or medium stacks up against others. See also *cost per contact,* and *CPM.*

Ellipsis.   A series of three dots (. . .) used to indicate deletions in quoted material. Also used for stylistic purposes to connect independent thoughts within a single sentence.

Emboss: Any shape that is impressed (raised) into a paper's surface. See *deboss* and *die.*

Em Quad.   A typesetting measure equal to the square of the type body of a capital M of a given face. Often used to indicate *indentation.* See also *en quad.*

En Quad.   A typesetting measure which is half an *em quad.*

Fact Sheet.   Literature designed to provide product details on a single sheet of paper. Also called *product* sheet or *spec sheet.*

Features.   Product specifications and attributes. Contrast to *benefits.*

Flat Color.   Opaque color inks which are used alone and not combined with other inks to produce other colors. Contrast to *process color.*

Flyer.   A sheet of printed material used as a handout. See also *broadside.*

Focus Group.   A market research technique which brings together a group of individuals to discuss their impressions of a given item or product.

Folio.   A page number.

Font.   All the letters, figures, punctuation marks, and so forth, of a single *typestyle* in a single size.

Format.   A particular *layout* style involving certain dimensions, the placement of elements, colors, etc. Usually established for a series of literature pieces.

Four-Color Process.   Full-color printing, arrived at by printing four *process* colors that combine visually to produce a full-color spectrum.

French Fold.   A double fold in which the sheet is folded once vertically and once horizontally.

Frequency.   The number of times a promotion runs during a particular time period.

Fulfillment. The process of fulfilling a request, usually for more information.

Galleys. Proofs of typeset matter not yet made up into pages.

Gate. A fold-out page or panel.

Ghost. A weak image, repeated from above or below, which appears in the middle of a heavily inked area on a printed sheet.

Graphic. Any distinctive character, symbol, or drawing.

Gravure. One of three popular printing processes— *letterpress, lithography,* and *gravure.* Prints from a series of line or dots recessed in the printing plate. Also called intaglio. Used mostly for very long runs and high quality.

Grid. A pattern established by a designer to make the layout of a literature piece easier, and its communication quicker.

Greek. Random letters put on a layout page to simulate the appearance of *type.*

Gutter. The division between two facing pages.

Halftone. Any printed photograph. Derives from the fact that to print a simulation of continuous tone, photographs must be broken into a series of small dots (half-tones). Contrast to *continuous tone.*

Hand Composition. The process of manually setting individual characters of *type* into lines.

Hard Copy. Any electronically stored material printed out on paper or film.

Hook. A written or visual device used to attract and hold the reader's interest.

Horizontal. Any item designed to reach a very wide audience of diverse interests.

House Organ. See also *house magazine.*

House Magazine. Any company-sponsored periodical with an editorial emphasis on feature articles.

Impact. The measurement of the persuasive power of a literature piece.

Impression. To a reader, the subjective feeling that comes from a literature piece. To a printer, the laydown of one layer of ink.

Imprint Space. Space left for a dealer or agent to print his own name and address or message.

Indention. The space left before the first word at the beginning of a paragraph. Flush indention means no indention. Regular indention is normally one or two em quads. Hanging indention means the first paragraph of a copy block is not indented, but every succeeding paragraph is.

Initial.   A large single character used for decoration at the beginning of a paragraph.

Insert.   Literature prepared for inserting between the pages of a publication.

Instruction Book.   Literature which explains how to use a product or service.

Intaglio.   See *gravure.*

Justification.   Adding space between words or letters to make a line of *type* fill a specified measure.

Layout.   An artist's rendition of what the literature will look like. See also *art.*

Lead-In.   The highlighted first few words of a paragraph or section of text.

Leading.   The spacing between typeset lines. Derives from the small strips used to separate lines when *type* is set in metal. Usually referred to as "*x points* leading."

Letterpress.   The printing process which prints from raised metal coming in direct contact with paper. Formerly very popular, now used mostly for imprinting and very high quality *type* and line illustrations. See also *gravure* and *lithography.*

Letterspacing.   Inserting space between letters to justify a line or improve its appearance. See also *wordspacing.*

Line Art.   All nonphotographic illustrations. Derives from the fact that such illustrations are composed of a series of lines of various widths.

Lithography.   The most widely used of the three popular printing processes—*gravure, letterpress* and *lithography.* Utilizes flat plates which are exposed to photographic films and are chemically sensitized to accept ink. See also *offset.*

Live Matter.   The printed area. It should be kept sufficiently within the trim to avoid any possibility of being cut off (except as desired). See also *bleed.*

Logo.   A characteristic symbol or signature, usually for an organization. Derives from logotype, a symbol set on a separate piece of *type.*

Makeready.   The activity in printing of getting a job on press ready to print.

Makeup. Putting the page elements—*type* and illustrations—together in a *mechanical.*

Manuscript. Final copy, ready to be typeset.

Measure. A *typesetting* term defining the length of a typeset line.

Mechanical. The page which the printer will photograph to make the plates from which to print.

Moire. An undesirable pattern that occurs in a halftone illustration when screen angles aren't proper, or when a previously screened illustration is rescreened.

Newsletter. Any small periodical, usually directed to a specific group, whose editorial emphasis is news.

Objective. A statement of purpose or intent, usually written down. Most communications work better when they are formulated to achieve certain objectives.

Offset. Generally accepted term for the modern *lithography* printing process. Also, the printback from undried ink onto a facing sheet.

Orphan. An excessively short last line of a page. See also *widow.*

Outline. A collection of information and facts organized for clarity to tell a story.

Overlay. A tissue placed over artwork or a *mechanical* to protect and allow reviewers to indicate changes and instructions.

Paid Circulation. A term which describes *house magazines* or *newsletters* which are for sale and are not restricted in their distribution. Contrast to *controlled circulation.*

Penetration. The extent to which the literature is seen by its potential audience. For example, 50 percent of potential readership equals 50 percent penetration. See also *reach.*

Perfecting Press. One that prints both sides of a sheet almost simultaneously.

Pica. A printer's unit of measurement. Often used to indicate the length of typeset lines. To find the length in inches divide picas by 6; to convert inches to picas, multiply by 6. (6 picas make one inch.)

PMS. An abbreviation for Pantone Matching System, a popular method of specifying flat color by means of numbered color samples which are available in swatchbooks.

Point. A printer's unit of measurement. 12 points make one *pica,* 6 picas make an inch. Also a definition of weight used for cover stock.

Point of Purchase (POP) Aids. Items used where the customer purchases to encourage him or her to make an immediate decision.

Positioning.   The process of identifying or establishing a unique spot or position for a product in the marketplace.

Presentation Book.   A loose-leaf binder or booklet which is used by a salesperson to summarize a sales presentation.

Press Release.   A bulletin outlining a new or significant event, sale, promotion, or new product. An excellent way to get free *publicity*.

Press Proof.   A proof sheet printed on the same press that will be used to print the job, versus one printed on a special proof press.

Process Color.   Transparent inks—usually cyan, magenta, and yellow—which, when overprinted, allow the reproduction of a full spectrum of color. Contrast to *flat color.*

Product Sheets.   Literature designed to provide product details on a single sheet of paper. See also *fact sheets* and *spec sheets.*

Production.   The physical process of getting the literature produced after all the creative work has been done.

Progressives.   Press proofs, in varying combinations, of each of the four separation halftones which make up a printed color illustration. They are used to show why a color reproduction may not be showing colors accurately.

Reach.   The number or percentage of individuals who have been exposed to a specific literature piece during a given time period.

Reminder Advertising.   Pens, key chains, calendars and other novelty items designed to keep the name of a business in front of customers.

Rivers.   Word spaces which appear to be connected vertically throughout a page, giving the appearance of a river of white space running through a grey page.

Roman.   Generic name for *type* with *serifs,* the most common type for reading. Contrast to *sans serif.*

Sales Promotion.   Activities which are designed to increase the sales of products through special events— promotions, contests, displays, etc. One of several promotional media.

Sans Serif.   Type without serifs. Contrast to *roman.*

Screening.   The process of converting a *continuous tone* photograph or illustration into *halftone* films.

Self-Cover.   Any literature piece in which the paper used for the text also is used for the cover.

Separations.   The four films, each representing a primary color, into which color photographs are converted for printing.

Serif.   The fine lines at the end of a character.

Sheet-Fed Press. A printing press which prints one sheet at a time. Usually results in the highest quality. Contrast to *web press.*

Sidebar. Text which appears outside the normal text, usually in an adjacent box or separate column. Used to separate out material which is related to a story line but not essential to it.

Size. Literature size is always stated as width by depth. For example, 9 × 12 means 9 inches wide by 12 inches deep.

Sketch. A rough *layout.*

Spec Sheet. Literature designed to provide product specifications on a single sheet of paper. Also called *product sheet* or *fact sheet.*

Stripping. The process of combining various pieces of film—*halftones, type,* etc.—into one master film for platemaking.

Stuffer. A small sheet designed primarily to be stuffed in an envelope along with a monthly billing statement.

Substance. The weight of paper. See also *basis.*

Surprint. Words printed over an illustration.

Thumbnail. A miniature-sized, very rough *layout.*

Tissue. See *overlay.*

Trade Customs. A set of printing industry standards which detail certain responsibilities and rights of a printer and his client. (See Appendix Two.)

Trademark/Tradename. A symbol or name registered by the United States Patent Office for the exclusive use of the registrant.

Type. The individual letters of the *copy,* ready to print.

Typography. The process of selecting, arranging and using *type.*

Typesetting. The process of converting the typewritten or handwritten copy into letters that will print.

Typestyle. One of the hundreds of thousands of letter designs available for the printed page.

Saltprint. See *brownline.*

Stat. Short for photostat. A photographic copy of the layout or mechanical.

Stock. Paper.

USP (Unique Selling Proposition). A phrase invented by adman Rosser Reeves to describe the process of focusing communication upon a product's single most important benefit to the customer.

Varnish. A lacquer applied to printed pages or sections of pages to make them glossy or to protect the ink from scuffing.

Vertical.   Any item designed to reach a very select audience with narrowly defined interests.

Web Press.   A high-speed printing press which prints on a continuous web of paper rather than on individual sheets. Can be more economical for high print runs. Contrast to *sheet-fed* press.

Weight.   Relative heaviness or thickness. Often used to describe *type.* Also the heaviness of a particular type of paper. See also *basis*.

Widow.   The last line of a paragraph with only one word or a part of a word. See also *orphan.*

PART Four

Appendixes

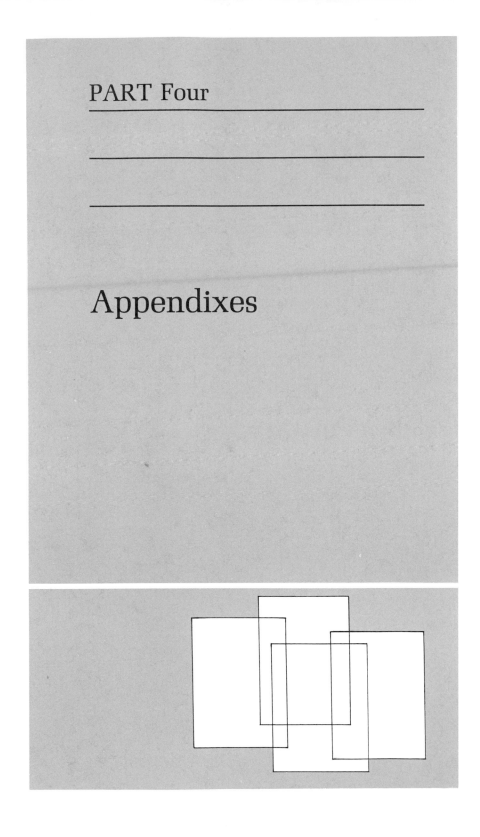

Appendix One

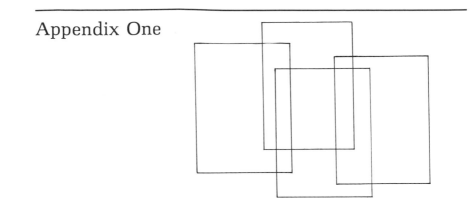

Tips and Techniques for Project Managers and Creative Staff

TEN WAYS TO BE A BETTER CREATIVE SUPPLIER

1. Be candid and precise on how you work, what you expect, and how you bill.
2. Do your homework *before* the first client meeting. Know enough to ask intelligent questions.
3. Be enthusiastic about the product, and let the client know it.
4. Remember the objectives of the literature. Never let creativity become more important than meeting the objectives.
5. Look beyond the obvious for a creative approach that will make the literature really stand out.
6. Put any daring or unusual creative ideas into your first effort. After that, follow the client's specific desires closely.

7. Be professional at all times. Act and look businesslike. Do what you promised, when you promised.
8. Don't begrudge the client his creative input. It's his product and his money.
9. Accept even nitpicking changes with grace. Remember, you are well paid for what you are doing.
10. Stay with the job all the way to the end. If you're a copywriter, read the mechanicals for typos; if you're a designer, check the binding as well as the presswork.

FIVE WAYS TO GET FASTER AND BETTER APPROVALS

Most creative people dread the review process, that time during which the draft copy and layout is circulated within an organization for comments, criticisms, and, ultimately, approval or disapproval. It is, however, a necessary process in any commercial creativity, and the more detail-intensive a project is, the more important it becomes. Considering the necessity of the process, what can be done to make approvals faster and easier, and to ensure better results? Far too often, the process (sometimes referred to as "disapproval" routing) simply slows things down and hinders creativity. Here are five ways a project manager can assure that this does not happen:

1. Make it a formal process. If you want a professional response, be professional in your request. Haphazard procedures invite haphazard reviews. Have approval routing forms printed; attach them to folders that include the material to be reviewed and all other relevant material. Establish a routing list and procedure. Make sure there is a procedure for noting comments and for filing them away for six months in case questions later arise.

2. Minimize the number of reviewers. When you ask someone for an opinion, you have to pay attention to what is said. But the more opinions you get, the better the chances the project will end up suffering from "committee think." So it's usually better not to ask. *Seldom should a literature piece be reviewed by more than half a dozen individuals.* Fewer is better. Select only one representative from each important function—product planning, sales, legal, distribution, corporate, and so forth. Don't let all parties comment on all issues; for example, restrict technical staff to checking technical facts. If the list of reviewers grows too long, try breaking it down into two separate lists: one "for approval" and one "for information only."

3. Circulate untouched copies. By making sure that a reviewer sees a clean, untouched copy, you can erect a strong psychological barrier to the impulse to make minor changes, without affecting the desire to correct errors of substance or style. Do this by circulating multiple copies for simultaneous review. True, this way one reviewer doesn't benefit from the comments of a previous one, but how often does this really help? And by circulating multiple copies, considerable time is saved.

4. Insist on keeping to a schedule. Determine a realistic time during which the material is to be reviewed by an individual (three or four days at most) and stick to it. On the due date, collect the material, or make sure it has been passed on, appropriately signed and dated. Adherence to deadlines can be an effective way to prevent procrastination. Keeping the pressure on also makes sure the material doesn't get misplaced, and is a demonstration of its importance.

5. Insist on editorial discretion. There is nothing more potentially damaging to the integrity of creative material than the reviewer who takes the liberty of injecting idiosyncrasies. The reviewer who disapproves of a cover because he or she doesn't like green or who removes "and" whenever it appears at the beginning of a sentence should rightfully be treated as an impediment to the review process and ignored. The project manager should also have the freedom to choose between conflicting views of style. When there is a consensus among reviewers that the style—either copy or art—is wrong, it should be communicated as specifically as possible to the creative team without attempting to dictate the fix.

Appendix Two

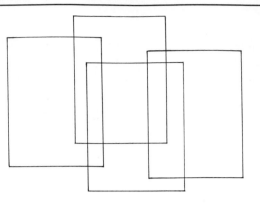

Printing Trade Customs

Printing is a venerable craft around which a number of business practices have grown up over the years. These practices have been codified by the printing industry in the publication of a list of trade customs. Some printers claim to obey them to the letter; some only certain ones; some none at all. In practice, however, all the industry is affected to some degree by the trade customs, and they are sometimes used as the basis for the settlement of disputes.

Anyone purchasing printing should be familiar with the trade customs and should obtain a statement from each printer used as to which, if any, will be enforced. Particular attention should be paid to the custom regarding overruns and underruns (#9 in the following list), since it is the cause for many misunderstandings. For example, to understand the impact of the custom concerning overruns and underruns, consider what happens when 10,000 brochures are absolutely needed. Because the printer can, according to the stated trade custom, legitimately deliver 10 percent less than this quantity, or 9,000 brochures

(10,000 − 10 percent), the purchaser will probably order 10 percent more, or 11,000 brochures, to ensure that his needs will be met. If, then, the printer actually delivers 10 percent more than the order—which, again, is legitimate according to the custom—the purchaser actually winds up with 12,100 brochures (11,000 plus 10 percent) which he must pay for.

Such customs, which evolved at a time when printing was less precise than it is today, have been subject to many abuses over the years. For this reason it is very appropriate for every purchaser of printing to consider each of the customs negotiable.

PRINTING TRADE CUSTOMS*

1. **Orders** regularly entered cannot be cancelled except upon terms that will compensate against loss.

2. **Experimental work** performed at customer's request, such as sketches, drawings, composition, plates (including lithographic plates), presswork, and materials shall be charged for at current rates.

3. **Sketches, copy dummies** and all preparatory work created or furnished by the printer, shall remain his exclusive property and no use of same shall be made, nor may ideas obtained therefrom be used, except upon compensation to be determined by the owner.

4. **Art work, type, plates** (including lithographic plates), engravings, electrotypes, negatives, positives, and other items when supplied by the printer shall remain his exclusive property, unless otherwise agreed in writing.

5. **Alterations:** Proposals are only for work according to the original specifications. If through customer's error, or change of mind, work has to be done a second time or more, such extra work will carry an additional charge, at current rates for the work performed.

6. **Standing type matter,** plates and negatives will not be held after completion of order except by special agreement and charge therefor.

7. **Proofs:** Two proofs shall be submitted with original copy. Corrections, if any, to be made thereon and to be returned marked "O.K." or "O.K. with corrections" and signed with name or initials of person duly authorized to pass on same. If revised proofs are desired, request must be made when proof is returned. Printer is not responsible for errors if work is printed as per customer's O.K.

---

* Courtesy of Printing Industries of America.

8. **Press proofs:** An extra charge will be made for press proofs, unless the customer is present when the form is made ready on the press, so that no press time is lost. Prepress standing awaiting O.K. of customer will be charged at current rates for the time so consumed.

9. **Overruns** or underruns not to exceed 10 percent of the amount ordered shall constitute an acceptable delivery and the excess or deficiency shall be charged or credited to the customer proportionately.

10. **Customer's property:** The printer shall charge the customer, at current rates, for handling and storing customer's stock or customer's printed matter held more than thirty (30) days. All customer's property that is stored with a printer is at the customer's risk, and the printer is not liable for any loss or damage thereto caused by fire, water leakage, theft, negligence, insects, rodents, or any cause beyond the printer's control. It is understood that the gratuitous storage of customer's property is solely for the benefit of the customer.

11. **Delivery:** Unless otherwise specified the price quoted is for a single shipment. F.O.B. customer's local place of business. All proposals are based on continuous and uninterrupted delivery of complete order, unless specifications distinctly state otherwise.

12. **Terms:** Net cash thirty (30) days. All claims must be made within five days of receipt of goods.

13. **Delays in delivery:** All contracts are made contingent upon wars, strikes, fires, floods, accidents, or other contingencies beyond the printer's control.

14. **Repairs, changes,** trimming, mortising, anchoring, special proving, or similar work required on materials which are furnished by the customer, including but not limited to drawings, engravings, electrotypes, and negatives, shall be billed at current market rates.

15. **Paper stock** furnished by the customer shall be properly packed, free from dirt, grit, turn sheets, bad splices, etc., and of proper quality for printing requirements. Additional cost due to delays or impaired production on account of improper packing or quality shall be charged to the customer.

16. **Color proofing:** Because of the difference in equipment and conditions between the color printing and the pressroom operations, a reasonable variation in color between color proofs and the completed job shall constitute an acceptable delivery.

Appendix Three

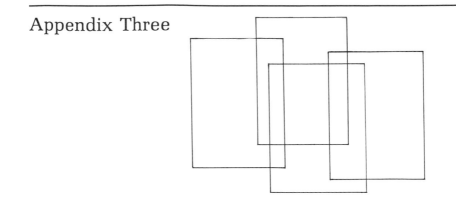

Proofreading Marks

Insert comma	⌃	Align	⸗
Insert apostrophe	⌄	Insert space	#
Insert quotation marks	⌄⌄	Hair space between letters	hr sp
Insert period	⊙	Push down space	⊔
Insert colon	⊙	Move to left	⊏
Insert semicolon	;/	Move to right	⊐
Insert question mark	?/	Lower	⊔
Insert hyphen	=/	Elevate	⊓
One-em dash	+	Broken letter	×
Two-em dash	⹀	Spell out (U S)	sp
En dash	⹀	Let it stand (some day)	stet
Ellipsis	l.l.l.l	Wrong font	wf
Delete	℘	Set in boldface type	bf
Close up	⌒	Set in roman type	rom
Delete and close up	ℨ	Set in italic type	ital
Reverse, upside-down	9	Small capitals	sc
Insert (caret)	∧	Capitals	caps
Paragraph	¶	Set in lower case	lc
No paragraph, run in	∾ ¶	Insert lead between lines	/ld⟩
Transpose (ther only is)	tr		

Appendix Four

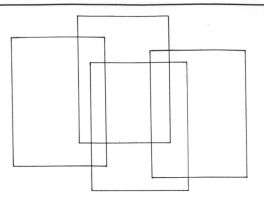

Putting More Muscle in an
Annual Report*

If I asked you to name the most cost-efficient and important communications medium a growing company has, chances are annual and quarterly reports wouldn't spring readily to mind. Advertising, with its measurable impact to offset expenditures, perhaps. Public relations, with a small budget and relatively large impact, more likely. But seldom, very seldom, is adequate attention given to the company's annual report.

Annual reports are one area where perception usually mirrors an unfortunate truth: Too often they are a high-cost, low-efficiency, but necessary corporate indulgence. And the smaller a company is, the more often than not this is apt to be true.

Of course, this shouldn't, and needn't, be so. When properly handled, an annual report can be the single most efficient medium a small-to-medium sized company has for positioning itself for future growth.

---

* By Cameron S. Foote. As it originally appeared in *Financial Executive* magazine.

The reason is simply because any growing company's future profitability depends to a large extent upon two very basic conditions: acceptance by the investing public, and acceptance by its customers. How a company goes about winning these acceptances should be very similar in both cases.

Think of it this way. Any company's growth depends upon financial, product, and marketing strategies. They need to be evaluated from time to time, and an annual review, of the type that results in a formal operations plan, is considered by most better-managed companies to be critically important in defining yearly activities and priorities.

Annual report preparation can both help structure and borrow from this yearly process if it is set up so that the report's editorial (as opposed to financial) source materials come directly from the operations plan. That way, the report's deadline pressure not only forces a tighter schedule upon the company's planning cycle, but, most likely, it will also result in the report containing the editorial material most recipients want to read—a version of the company's strategy for the year(s) ahead. The net result of this dual use of information is one of those rarities in business: better internal planning and better external communications.

There is also another advantage of combining the information-gathering of the two activities, and that is the opportunity for a better writing and presentation style to rub off on the operations plan. And if no yearly planning cycle exists in the company, the need for a formal strategy statement for the annual report is a good way to prod one into existence.

From this solid base of confidential fact and strategy the focus of the year's annual report can be easily and rationally determined. It can then be tailored to externally position the company to fit whatever long-term strategy goals are deemed to be important.

Once the report's focus is determined, emphasis can be put on giving it the type of visual impact and readability that will mark it as being from a growing, dynamic and sophisticated company. And make no mistake, impact and sophistication are very important in gaining the attention of the potentially influential annual report reader. Each year, literally dozens of annual reports cross the desk of a typical financial analyst. Only those of interest are noted at all. And, usually, only those with a well-presented story can affect in a positive way an objective analyst's opinion of a company.

TWO REPORT APPROACHES

Take Company "A," a leader in a small, highly sophisticated segment of the electronics industry. Each year for the past three, its market share has been slowly eroding, and so has the price of the stock. To counteract this, the Board made a major decision to heavily increase the company's commitment to applied research. The details are in the company's yearly confidential operations plan, and the expenditures will show up publicly in the annual report's financial section. But full benefit from this action will come only when presented in such a way as to instill share-owner confidence and attract new investors.

Both were accomplished by an annual report designed to emphasize the company's research activity, and which contained a message by the vice president of research that detailed recent breakthroughs and quoted part of the operations plan. The total effect was a hard-to-ignore positive statement; it was made further credible by the financial data, and played a strong role in building investor confidence.

Company "B" had a different problem, but one equally responsive to being addressed through the annual report. All financial data were positive, but the company was having trouble attracting the highly qualified professional staff that its business of supplying long-term contractual services depended upon. And it had a constant need to publicize how its dedicated employees provided outstanding service.

Noting that the annual report was used extensively by both the personnel department and sales force to profile the company and its services, a decision was made to orient the report around a strong visual theme that would focus on the attractiveness of the company's work life.

The strategy proved eminently successful. It gave a big boost to employee morale, accelerated the recruitment program, and sent a strong quality-control leadership message to customers who find an annual report the most credible means of assessing a company's long-term dependability. As a side benefit, it also attracted a new level of interest by the financial community.

These two examples show but two ways that any company, through assessing its weaknesses and strengths, can use its annual report to go considerably beyond the legal requirements of financial reporting. Simply put, because an annual report is required of all New York Stock Exchange and American Stock Exchange listed corporations, as well as many over-the-counter traded corporations, it makes considerable economic sense not to waste this valuable and expensive opportunity on anything less than reinforcing a company's strengths and addressing its weaknesses. Best of all, doing so usually costs very little more. Better effectiveness is usually a simple matter of better planning, strategy, and creativity.

Similarly, a company's quarterly financial reports can also be an effective and logical means of following up and extending the annual report message. The quarterly report can double as an investor newsletter to highlight new company products and services. In any case, quite often spending a third of so more on quarterly report preparation can make it up to three times more effective.

Unincorporated companies and closely held corporations may want to look at the advantages of producing an "annual review." With up to 60 percent of most small-to-medium-size company reports actually used for nonfinancial purposes—everything from recruiting personnel to showing product applications—producing a review/report may be very productive, even though not required. Its official nature will give it much more credibility than a normal capability brochure. Plus, if the company later goes public, the mechanism for producing effective annual reports will already be in place.

To assure that your annual report preparation is approached from the most cost effective standpoint, here are three rules to keep in mind.

DEFINE, YEARLY, A CORPORATE COMMUNICATIONS STRATEGY

Make this strategy the editorial theme of your annual and quarterly reports. Don't waste a valuable opportunity by choosing a theme that merely satisfies the corporate ego or the chairman's fancy; be ruthlessly pragmatic. The theme can be related to finance, product, personnel, or any other subject. What's important is that behind it stands a well-reasoned strategy that's been carefully reviewed, that's in sync with the corporation's operations plan, and that will be reinforced by the financial figures reported.

BE INFORMATIVE AND INTERESTING

An annual report is the single most important printed document most companies regularly produce. For any company, it reflects financial health, a perception of self, and a view of the future. And for newer, smaller firms, it may also be the principal reference for potential investors. For these reasons, many companies already realize the value of a good graphic designer to lay out the report. Yet, very few will also call in professional writing help, preferring to let that assignment be fragmented and sandwiched between the other tasks of the company president and the public relations staff. And many companies also try to economize by using photography taken from public relations files and ad campaigns. It just does not work to insist on quality in only one part of the creative process.

A good, effective annual report is always the effort of two complementary teams: an in-house communications/executive staff to set strategy, gather material, produce a budget, and provide clearances; an outside writer/designer/photographer team to give the material the impact and interest only objective professionals, working together on a schedule and budget, can produce.

SPEND WHERE IT COUNTS, CUT BACK WHERE IT DOESN'T

Does employing all this outside help actually run up the cost? The answer is yes. But probably less than you think. Although it's difficult to profile a typical annual report expense, on average, only about 25 percent of total expenditures for a small-to-medium size company's annual report are for the creative services used in preparation. And the incremental difference between first-rate and mediocre creativity will probably never be more than 10 percent. On an annual report estimate of $85,000 (a realistic figure for 25,000 24-page reports), that's an incremental expense of just $8,500. Put another way, for just $8,500 more per year, an ineffective or mediocre company representative can he replaced with one that's absolutely topnotch.

Creative services, then, are not usually the place to apply the budget tourniquet. Nor is the selection of a good printer, one who can get out of the design and photography all of its built-in potential.

The way a job is scheduled is usually the single best way to reduce annual report costs. Annual report preparation and printing is a highly seasonal industry that builds to a crescendo of activity in the 90 days following the close of fiscal years on December 31 and June 30. Any work scheduled in the 90 days prior to each of these dates is usually in an off-peak time and can be obtained for less money.

For example, the theme can be decided, the editorial matter written, the design done, the photography taken, and the prepress work started and held at the printer long before the close of the fiscal year. Then, when the financial figures are released after the year's closing, they can be rushed to the printer and the whole job put on press a few days later.

By scheduling writer / designer / photographer / typesetter / printer in off-peak time, an overall savings of 20 percent or more can be realized. Most likely, this will allow you to obtain topnotch creative talent and still save money over previous efforts. Plus, there will be a better selection of creative talent to choose from. And even more important, you'll probably also avoid the single biggest cause of annual report cost overruns—the overtime necessary to get the job printed and in the mail prior to the stock exchange's deadline. (For NYSE-listed companies, 15 days before the annual meeting, but not later than 90 days after close of the fiscal year. For AMEX-listed companies, 10 days before the annual meeting, but not later than 120 days after close of the fiscal year. OTC companies need only adhere to state laws.)

For maximum efficiency, plan to select your annual report creative team and printer about five months before the report needs to be delivered. Make a final decision on a theme and layout with four months to go. Expect all creative work to be done two months ahead of time. Allow one month for printing and distribution.

SUMMARY

Do all you can to keep your annual and quarterly reports strategically positioned, creatively exciting, and financially efficient. Preparation does not have to be traumatic, nor extravagant, but it must be effective.

An annual report should work hard for your company every single day of this year and many years into the future, whether or not your firm ever grows into a corporate giant. In fact, it may surprise you to learn that several Fortune 100 companies do, indeed, follow the procedure given above, as well as some of their own making, to keep both quality up and costs down.

After all, regardless of a corporation's size, annual and quarterly reports are always something of a paradox: something just too important to scrimp on, and something just too costly not to be done right.

Appendix Five

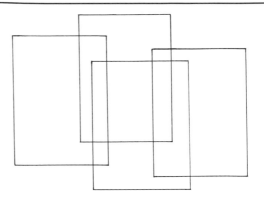

Analyzing Media?
Don't Forget Your
House Organ*

If you're at all typical, chances are you see dozens of media representatives each year. You consult with them, you challenge them. You agonize over demographics, audits, costs per thousand, editorial direction.

Then you get the advice of your agency's media director, who has gone through exactly the same thing. You do all this because you know how important it is to make sure that your company's space advertising money is spent in the most cost-effective way. Yet, for all this emphasis on media analysis, it never seems to touch what can be the most underanalyzed, inefficiently utilized medium in industrial marketing—the house organ, newsletter, or other company publication.

One reason is that company publications often come about in a rather unusual fashion. Typically, one day someone in management (maybe even you) discovers that: (1) the company has

---

* By Cameron S. Foote. As it originally appeared in *Industrial Marketing* magazine.

more to say than can be said in paid space; and (2) the company will probably get more "reach" for the money with its own publication anyway. What results can be as simple as a monthly newsletter to customers, or as sophisticated as a lavishly- printed magazine sent to a larger segment of the business community. In any case, it seems henceforth to elude any objective analysis.

It need not be so. Whether your company's marketing publications were conceived in this fashion or more rationally, there are ground rules that will let you evaluate their current performance. You will not have media representatives to help, but if properly done there will be no one more competent to challenge your analysis, either. And you may just end up recommending a way to save your company some money.

ANALYZE THE CONTENT

The first thing to remember when analyzing or considering a marketing house magazine or newsletter is that they represent a totally different type of communications medium. Unlike print advertising there is none of the focus or third party editorial surround to lend objectivity and guarantee a certain amount of readership. And unlike commercial magazines, to which erroneous comparisons often are made, they lack the editorial objectivity, polish, and variety readers expect.

Commercial magazines exist, after all, to provide a forum by which ideas, sometimes conflicting, can reach a homogeneous group. A magazine's success is determined solely by how well its readers and advertisers feel it fulfills that role.

A house magazine, on the other hand, exists to sell something the company has made or done. Its success is determined solely by how well it performs that function. If constructed editorially like a commercial magazine, it wouldn't sell a thing, and should be judged a failure. So, too, should one that tries to sell like an ad—the style is wrong for the medium.

What, then, is the right content? A successful company magazine always contains either: (1) news—new developments presented so that the reader feels a personal involvement in the future of the product or services; or (2) instruction—techniques and products which show the reader how to save time and money. Nothing else.

This is not the place for corporate chauvinism, nor for the president to expound on his political views.

And the sales manager shouldn't make it an extension of the field sales force—i.e., a homey mixture of sales pitch and BS—either. This is indeed a place to sell, but in a rather different manner.

When analyzing the content of company publications, consider first how well they address reader interests.

If they contain product news and information that are of genuine interest to the reader they pass this simple test. If not, your company is wasting its money.

This was brought home to me rather succinctly a few years ago when I was the proud young editor of a company house organ. On a field call, I asked a rather grizzled old tradesman what he thought of the magazine I published.

He thought for a while, then replied, "I've got to be honest with you. I read only two types of things: at home, that which I enjoy; on the job what which helps me. Unfortunately, your magazine is neither."

ANALYZE THE STYLE

Style, of course, is intimately linked to content. It certainly is just as important, too, for company magazines (whether we like to consider them as such or not) are really a form of direct mail, and like all direct mail, start out with two strikes against them.

Regardless of whether or not they are requested, they have rather low reader desire. On top of that, they must fight for attention with a myriad of other items (including other company magazines) that the postman dumps daily on the reader's desk.

House magazines must be visually inviting and offer stimulating reading regardless of how good their content may be. If not, they don't stand a chance. This is not to say that they have to be elaborate (that, too, can often be self-defeating) but this is not the place to scrimp, either. If you do, more than likely you'll end up writing for an audience of one—yourself.

Also, consider that any company publication, even a small-circulation newsletter to an obscure market, reflects upon the company at large. A number of such poorly done newsletters can do a great deal to unmake years of calculated effort to up-grade your company's market position.

In spite of all this, it is a regrettable fact that the most common justification for house magazines is their inexpensiveness. "All we have to do," the reasoning goes, "is get the engineers to contribute the words, let the ad manager polish them up and run off and mail the copies." Inexpensive, yes. Effective, no.

The next thing you crank into your analysis, then, is whether or not your house magazines exhibit proven, professional communications skills—appropriate style, good writing, strong graphics,adherence to deadlines, etc. If they do, they meet one more of the criteria for effectiveness. If not, more than likely they will be ineffective, regardless of how well they meet other criteria.

AUDIENCE AND MARKET POSITION

Since most of us are governed by our own self-interest, house magazines can nearly always do well where the audience is to some degree captive and feels an obligation to read— salespeople, dealers, representatives, etc. Such publications provide a means of self-preservation through telling us what is going on in the marketplace, or "back at the home office." If a publication is aimed at this audience, it cannot miss when well prepared.

When it comes to customers, however, things are considerably different. His or her self interest is tied in only the most tenuous way to your company's objectives—and only if he or she knows and respects your company.

My experience tells me that well-prepared house magazines always are a good investment when used in a mature market where the firm has a strong reputation for quality goods and/or services. Conversely, they are nearly always ineffective when published by an unknown company in a mature market, or by any company in an immature market.

Company publications are effective when used by an industry leader as an inexpensive way of reinforcing an already established market position. The effectiveness of a well-prepared house publication will rise in direct relation to the company's market share and position.

A company trying to break into a market, or selling in a market that has determined no leaders (an immature market) does not have a position to reinforce. That company should concentrate on establishing a strong market position (leader in price, dependability, service, technology, etc.) as soon as possible.

And that job is more effectively done by using the more direct, hard-selling media—advertising and direct mail—which give a more rapid return on investment.

Thus, in your analysis, view your house publications as a communications vehicle to reinforce and extend your company's market position. If they are doing that job, give them high marks. If not, do some serious thinking about what, exactly, they are doing, and how much it really costs.

ANALYZING THE COSTS

How much should you spend? There is, of course, no simple answer, just a generalization: If your company is a market leader, any reasonable expenditure is a bargain.

Company magazines are the most inexpensive, cost-effective way to meet long-term sales and image goals. They can inform, instruct, and build loyalty for your company and its brands for a few dollars per customer, per year. Nothing is more efficient.

If, however, your company is not a market leader (and do try to think objectively about that) the amount of money necessary to produce a publication with market impact will normally be more than it's worth. Face up to it—there are just more efficient ways to sell.

Tally the personnel costs, too. Every publication needs a good editor. And editing even a quarterly newsletter can be a demanding, time-consuming job, albeit one with many rewards. Do not attempt publishing if you do not have the staff or budget. But do not shrink from getting them if you have the real need.

A boss of mine once gave me some sage advice about editing. "You won't make it as an editor," he said, "until you have learned to plan at least five issues ahead." Let me add that once you have mastered that significant feat, you also will know more than enough to give your house magazines the continuing analyses they need.

INDEX